Praise for *Seal, Sigil & Call*

"Spirituality is individuality, and J. R.'s book captures what so many of us are seeking: our own path. This collection of his personal spiritual experiences expressed in a complex, well-thought-out system guides those who would walk that path, but it also inspires. You can use this book to define and shape a ritual magical practice that is unique to you." —**Natalie Zaman, award-winning author of *Magical Destinations of the Northeast***

"*Seal, Sigil, and Call* is new light on an old topic. It offers novel and innovative perspectives, techniques, and new models to work practical magick... Don't let the seeming familiarity of some of the material fool you into thinking that it is a simple reworking of traditional lore. It is a new and coherent system with a different style and vision for developing your skills, communing with spirits, and working effective magick. There are many distinctive ideas and methods that you may wish to add to your tool kit, even if you don't adopt it as your primary system." —**Ivo Domínguez Jr., author of *The Four Elements of the Wise***

S·E·A·L
S·I·G·I·L
& C·A·L·L

About the Author

J. R. Mascaro is a sorcerer, meditation guide, and mindfulness advocate who has been engaged in the work of the magician since childhood. He has used his practice, detailed in this book, to navigate life during his time here on earth, which has taken him through varied avenues and locations on a journey of discovery. By way of day jobs, he has worked in entertainment, education, the arts, and technology. J. R. has employed his esoteric practice as a catalyst for self-cultivation, constantly seeking to outgrow old patterns and nurture new understanding. It is his fervent hope that this book will help others in their own personal journeys.

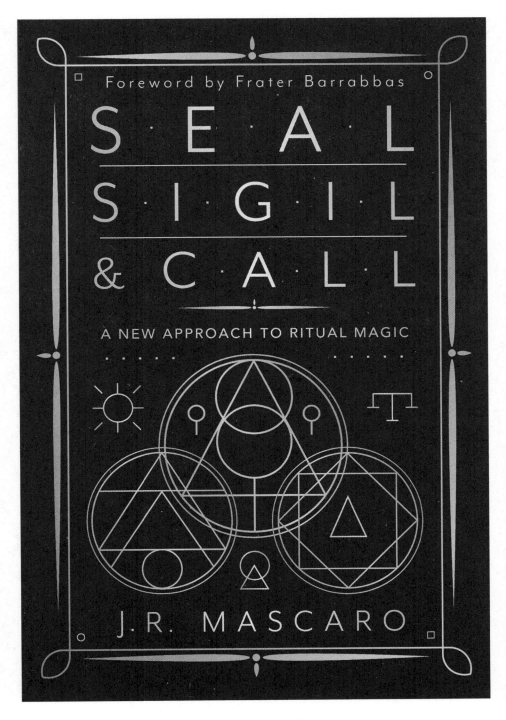

Foreword by Frater Barrabbas

S·E·A·L
S·I·G·I·L
&·C·A·L·L

A NEW APPROACH TO RITUAL MAGIC

J.R. MASCARO

Llewellyn Publications | Woodbury, Minnesota

FIRST EDITION
First Printing, 2022

Book design by Christine Ha
Cover design by Kevin R. Brown
Interior art by the Llewellyn Art Department (original concepts developed by author)

Llewellyn Publications is a registered trademark of Llewellyn Worldwide Ltd.

Library of Congress Cataloging-in-Publication Data (Pending)
ISBN: 978-0-7387-7053-6

Llewellyn Publications
A Division of Llewellyn Worldwide Ltd.
2143 Wooddale Drive
Woodbury, MN 55125-2989
www.llewellyn.com

Printed in the United States of America

For my mother, my sister, and my wife,
and in loving memory of my godfather.

CONTENTS

Contents

FOREWORD

There are many books being written and published on the topic of magic these days, and specifically the kind of magic that is accessible and that you can quickly start using. Most of them are based on the traditional practices of the Golden Dawn or some variation on that theme. Few of them are both innovative and cutting edge in how they present to the seeker a system of magic that is easy to acquire and doesn't necessitate purchasing a lot of material. That was true until this book came out.

Here is a book that is different from any other that you might seek to purchase. It is innovative but not dismissive of other traditions; it is cutting edge without being too novel or bogged down by excessive occult technology. It is a system of magic whose only requirements are an open mind, a fertile imagination, an ability to internally visualize, and a basic practice of meditation. The magic of *Seal, Sigil & Call* is a particular transcendental form of magic for the postmodern age.

J. R. was born in a small town in northeast New Jersey and was raised by a gifted, intelligent, and open-minded mother. He suffered acutely from ADHD, but being a very intelligent and precocious child, he discovered meditation at a young age and, by himself, found the means to control his impulsive nature and inability to focus. J. R. was a dreamy child who saw the world as if it were a theater presentation, where the day-to-day occurrences were somewhat unreal or allegory. He probably asked the kind of questions that shouldn't be asked or couldn't readily be answered, and so, at an early age, he began his quest for spiritual truth and answers to his endless questions.

While his years in school seemed to be wasted (and irrelevant), he had his great intellectual awakening when attending the university where he managed to excel, graduating with a BA in anthropology. When it came time for him to find work, he used his talents at learning new subjects to teach himself enough computer programming to get a job and thereafter found a career in IT.

All during this time, J. R. was accumulating knowledge and experience of the occult arts and sciences. Friendly and open-minded with others, he didn't join any traditional orders or groups, since he found all that he needed from a myriad of books and his continuous experimentation. J. R.'s approach to his studies of the occult was to deeply examine multiple disciplines and find common threads in them, determining for himself the touchstones of truth and then incorporating them into his work.

Since meditation was his first and foremost discipline, he used this practice as his foundation for developing a synthetic and hybrid system of magic. J. R. has an inherent skepticism about all things and needs to bring a subject or a technique into his personal sphere to ensure that it is factual and practically useful. This kind of application and experimentation has been brought into his book, so what he presents in it will be of practical use to the magical seeker.

The book *Seal, Sigil & Call* uses a twofold mechanism to bring the world of magic quickly and directly to the seeker. The first mechanism is where the body power-points are energized and centered, and then cleansed sacred space is empowered with the power of the elementals. The second mechanism uses a simplified version of evocation to summon and materialize a spirit entity known as an eidolon. The mediator of both mechanisms is the scepter of artifice, a tool representing a powerful conceptual device known as the scepter of the art, an emblem of one's projected will.

The eidolons are the core constituency of J. R.'s system of magic, and although they are left nameless, their seal and qualities represent archetypal intelligences found in nearly every tradition. For instance, the first eidolon is reminiscent of the pagan god Bacchus, or Dionysus. Still, it is up to the operator, who takes up this system of magic, to find the personal names and derive the sigils for these entities. While J. R. has gifted the reader with eighteen of these eidolons from his personal practice, there is a veritable possibility of a limitless number of such beings available to the operator to build a powerful system of magic, based on both an energy base and a container, or "ark," of spirits.

J. R. spends over a third of the book describing the eighteen foundational eidolons and the methods of contacting them, developing the *call*, and learning how to *listen* to their response. This is a system of magic with limitless possibilities to be acquired and built upon by the seeker of magic. It is an "open source" kind of magical system that invites the beginning magician to build their own personalized system of magic.

This book was written for those readers interested in magic, but who find themselves at odds with works written by traditional ceremonial magicians. They probably find themselves impatient with the doctrines and slow-paced requirements as found in traditional magical lodges. The self-taught, experiential, and practical-based seeker, who has not yet mastered a system of magic, will find this book to be very important, since it cuts through all of the unnecessary and hyperbolic claims and personal politics to reveal what is truly essential and foundational to the practice of magic.

J. R. reveals his compassionate nature throughout this book and shows his simple desire to help others to gain what he has gained over many years of study and experiment. I recommend that those who might be turned off or turned away by the media hype associated with many various personalities and traditions in today's practice of magic will find in this book the unalloyed and rarefied truth to build their own system of magic, which will help them to achieve an ultimate state of material and spiritual fulfillment, and perhaps even spiritual transcendence.

—*Frater Barrabbas*

INTRODUCTION

As far back as I can remember, for my entire life and a bit more besides, I have sought the key to the mysteries. I have pored over more books than I can number or name, many long out of print and excavated from the dusty shelves of small bookstores. I have sat with fellow seekers and explored esoteric avenues of ritual and ceremony. I have seen much I cannot put to words, but what I can articulate, I shall endeavor to share with you in this book.

Early on in my search, as but a child, I realized that I processed information differently than my peers. This neurodiversity, diagnosed differently throughout my life, would prove helpful, as well as hindering. On the one hand, my nonlinear thinking helped me to piece together the things I remembered and perceived outside of the temporal bounds of my incarnate existence. These memories and perceptions had me reading at a college level early in my life and led me to inquire into subjects I had not been introduced to in this lifetime. I was, and am, continuing a body of work begun before this incarnation. However, on the other hand, this way of receiving and processing information has made it difficult to orient myself in time and more difficult to keep my short-term memory in order when I am occupied with the many things I perceive aside from the physical world before my physical eyes. In addition, I have always possessed a notion that the world in which we find ourselves is something of a puppet show, that each of our bodies is but a receiver for our consciousness, and together we create this dream reality through some manner of collaborative storytelling. This innate belief made accepting materialist explanations for phenomena counterintuitive.

Due to this disinclination toward regimentation and disregard for the trappings of the physical world, I found many schools of ceremonial magic to be too formulaic and often confined by the sensibilities of the ages that birthed or interpreted them. There was much emphasis on the procurement of physical reagents or rote memorization of exact incantations. Chafing against these preoccupations with external conditions, I sought to chart my own way to some glimpse of gnosis. As the seventeenth-century Japanese poet Matsuo Basho once said, "Do not simply follow in the footsteps of the ancients; seek what they sought."[1]

With this spirit of self-illumination, I very quickly found myself off the rails of the mystical schools I had been exposed to. I have had the privilege of learning many modalities from an eclectic array of generous teachers, but I possess an internal wanderlust that rendered me unable to confine myself to a single approach of discovery. Due to this, I began to develop a syncretic approach to the esoteric, a cobbled together personal tradition that incorporated the most personally enriching and self-resonant elements of the various schools I had been exposed to. This would eventually coalesce into the system you now hold in your hands, which I refer to as paneidolism. This practice is named in this way due to the fact that it revolves around the detection of and communication with nonphysical intelligences known as eidolons, which are present around us at all times. In this way, this practice is a form of sorcery in the traditional sense of the word, insofar as it deals chiefly with communication with energetic beings.

To introduce some basic operating conditions of this practice, I will make several assertions that you are encouraged to engage with as you practice the exercises in this book and draw your own conclusions. These

---

1. Matsuo, *Narrow Road to the Interior and Other Writings*, Introduction.

assertions are as follows. The root level assertion of this practice is that the reality we engage in is itself conscious on a level we cannot comprehend. In addition, the nature of each sentient being is that of eternal, self-sovereign consciousness that exists independently from physical matter. This reality contains patterns that can be observed, influenced, and followed if one can learn to open their awareness to them. Thought is the primary agent of change upon existence and will is thought invested with direction and purpose. Magic is the name for the technique through which we may enact our will upon the metaphysical framework of existence. To aid us in the enactment of our will, we can enlist the help of nonphysical thoughtforms that exist within and/or beyond us, known as eidolons. Magic is to be used for the good of the collective, the vast network-of-being in which we all participate, and as such, it should never be used to harm other beings emotionally or physically, nor to oppress, enslave, or subjugate. Positive effect on the collective good can be enacted through directly helping those in need in this realm, working to dismantle injustice wherever it resides, and through engaging with the harmonious patterns of the multiverse and the tasks to which they may lead you. These tasks will often include interaction with conceptual entities, known as vestiges, and stagnations in energetic systems, called blockages. The total goal of the earthly magician is to transcend to a higher modality of discernment in order to engage fully with the work of magic beyond the fetters of the physical senses and to more deeply understand the nature of the conscious multiverse.

This book is meant to serve as a one-stop shop for learning to foster a mindset conducive to esoteric practice, engage in ritual, and eventually make successful contact with a group of eidolons I refer to as the inner host. This is accomplished through encouraging you to engage with your own presuppositions about reality, nurture a receptive and attuned mindset, and develop your own practice of ritual magic. It is important to note that this book encourages you to cultivate your own approach as you progress, and it is not meant to be taken dogmatically. This practice will be useful to you if you are seeking a framework around which to develop your own magical practice without being boxed in to overly restrictive or stifling requirements. Explore, experiment, and discover at your leisure.

This book is engineered to take you from a neophyte in this system, which, by virtue of this being the first book on paneidolism, you must be, to a practicing magician using the tools I have put forth. It will use common exercises gleaned from widespread esoteric modalities to introduce you to the concepts of energy and centered awareness and will quickly progress from there to the practices unique to this pursuit. These practices include learning to contact the eighteen eidolons specified in this book and, perhaps more importantly, learning to listen to the unique symphony of existence to discern the presence of infinite as-yet unspecified eidolons yourself.

Terminology Unique to This System

In the pages to follow, you will interact with new terms, as well as familiar terms that will have changed in the context of this work. In order to prevent confusion, I offer a short list of terms that will help you to navigate the following chapters.

ark: The overall collection of eidolon entries in your tome; it is the list of eidolons that you have made contact with or are beginning to become aware of.

eidolon: An independent thoughtform that you might interpret as a manifestation of your own subconscious or as an independent, externally extant intelligence inhabiting a nonphysical dimension.

emblem: Analogous to a spell, an emblem is called such as it is a marker of an agreement made with an eidolon; it is also a trigger to evoke a certain effect.

gate: A gate is a pattern used to create and sustain a lasting effect in a space or object.

inner host: The eighteen eidolons contained in this book and understood to be known by all magicians whose practices are based, however loosely, on the techniques found in this book.

nine gates: The philosophical gates a magician must pass through in the intention-setting ritual contained in this book, the Circle of Concentric Ascension. These represent the four material elements: air, fire, water, and earth; the four immaterial elements: light, darkness, life, and death; and the all-animating quintessential element: spirit.

octadecagon gate: The philosophical gate presided over by the eighteenth eidolon; the passing of it represents a magician beginning to work with new eidolons they discover themselves.

outer host: All eidolons in a magician's ark beyond the eighteen of the inner host.

scepter of art: A thought and visualization tool for directing the focus of thaumaturgical will.

scepter of artifice: A physical anchor point for the scepter of art.

tome: The book in which you keep all of your notes on your magical work, as well as your ark.

Using This Book

This book is meant to be read and the exercises within performed. It may benefit you to first read the entire book cover to cover in order to understand the journey and concepts within before beginning again and performing the techniques over the course of a year or more. It is your choice whether you wish to be preinformed, or to find out bit by bit over the course of your exploration.

In the first half of this book, in chapters 1 through 5, you will be presented with the foundational elements upon which you can build an entire practice. In these pages, we will discuss energy, intention, and the practice of working with eidolons that defines the core of paneidolism.

In the second half of this book, in chapters 6 through 8, we will discuss further cultivating the practices introduced earlier on to a new depth, learning to create your own techniques and rituals for daily use, and advanced work meant to be engaged with after time as a consistent practitioner.

Chapter 1
SETTING THE
CORNERSTONE

You are about to embark on a journey into the unknown, one that I hope will prove enriching. My goal is to provide a fertile substrate for you to cultivate in the terraforming of your own inner world. Before you begin this journey, you will require a journal to record your discoveries and a map by which you can orient yourself in the strange new worlds you may encounter. The journal is your tome, and the map, the north star by which you will find your way through various philosophical quandaries, is your operating paradigm.

Keeping Your Own Tome

First and foremost, this book does not exist simply to read. This book exists to aid you in the creation of your own book, a tome in which you will keep your notes on the paneidolic system that will be presented here and then expand upon as you develop your own practice on the foundation provided. While your tome can be any blank notebook, it is recommended that you invest in the sturdiest specimen you can locate. It is meant to last a literal lifetime. Indeed, in your pursuit of the work, you may fill many such tomes. A journal of the A5 size with a hard cover and thick 120g dotted paper is suggested. These parameters achieve a balance between portability and writing space and prevent ink bleed through. Dotted pages are equally suited to writing neatly and drawing and, as such, are superior to blank or lined paper for the purposes of the work. By way of writing instruments, several weights of archival ink pens are suggested to prevent fading over the years. For seal and sigil work, it is recommended you lightly draw in pencil first and then ink your work once you deem it satisfactory. A selection of basic geometry tools will also aid you here. You will find those most useful to be a ruler, compass, and protractor.

Your notebook can be called many things. Varied traditions may refer to such a book as a tome, a Book of Shadows, or a grimoire, among many other specialized terms. One of the first things that you must internalize is the inherent subjectivity of magic. There is no one "true" path for the magician, nor any single "true" title or toolbox. There are many paths and traditions that grasp at gnosis, and universal truths are not bound by linguistic classification. In the words of Khalil Gibran: "Say not, I have 'found the truth,' but rather 'I have found a truth.'"[2] You are free to call your working book whatever you like; simply be sure to take care of it.

As you progress in the methodologies introduced to you, you will find it of great value to take notes, not only on the concepts and exercises themselves presented but on your musings, reflections, and questions about them. Nearly every concept you encounter can be researched into further, and doing so is highly encouraged. After you complete the exercises, you should return to your book and note the feelings, sensations, thoughts, and inspirations gleaned through them. Your book can also be used to keep track of your meditations, dreams, or any other practice in which you engage to pursue higher consciousness or inner tranquility.

Establishing an Operating Paradigm

Once you have your working book selected and in hand, you are halfway to beginning the work set forth in the preceding pages, but before you do, it is vital that you possess a philosophical underpinning to provide a framework or lens through which you view the experiences to come. This is your operating paradigm.

---

2. Gibran, *The Prophet*, 55.

An operating paradigm is the core of your practice. It answers such questions as "How do I define magic?" and "Why am I engaging in this work?" An operating paradigm is nothing less than the assumption upon which your entire practice stands; you cannot deliberately practice the art of magic if you cannot define for yourself what it is and why you are engaged in it. With magic, intention is everything, and will is the sole necessary tool. All matter and energy is bound first by thought, and will is thought given purposeful direction. To have intention toward something, you must have a notion of that thing; you must have a clear vision in your mind upon which you may focus.

What is magic to you? How do you define it? There are many schools of thought you can explore to come to these answers, but it is best to start with a simple distinction. From there you are encouraged to explore further and take notes on your conclusions in your tome. The first distinction you must make is whether you believe the forces you engage with during magical practice are internal or external.

Defining a magical practice as internal is to state that you believe the forces with which you are engaging during magical work are metaphorical in nature. It is to posit that these intelligences are facets of your own subconscious or unconscious mind. They are allegorical thoughtforms you will use to organize your thoughts, realize your personal potential, and gain mastery over yourself.

Defining a magical practice as external is to state that you believe the forces with which you are engaging during magical work are metaphysical in nature and that they are actual extant entities that operate on a plane, or planes, outside of standard human vision.

As with many things in magic, the lines between these two approaches need not be solid. Magic is at home on the borders, and viewing the forces with which you work as both external and connected to your deeper self is not uncommon. Indeed, you may decide that separation between entities is in and of itself illusory.

Reflect on your definition of magic. From whence do you believe it derives its efficacy, inner reflection, or external forces? Take note of your thoughts on this in your tome, and perhaps reflect on whether they change after engaging in the exercises in the first section of this book. The practices we pursue in this book are not meant to be dogmatic or rigid. Your definitions and assumptions will shift. They will grow as you grow. As you progress upon your personal path as a magician, you will test hypotheses, grow past methodologies, and take part in the metaphorical cycle of death and rebirth—the death and rebirth of the ego. Like a serpent, you will slough off the dull shed of old ideas and expose the brilliant sheen of new thoughts and experiences. Do not become so attached to your practices that you cannot move on when they no longer serve you. Attachment is the anchor that drowns ascension.

The next question you must endeavor to answer is why you wish to pursue the art of magic. Why did you purchase, borrow, or otherwise procure this book? What do you believe magic can achieve for you? This is another question, like the last, that you may spend the rest of your life answering because it will change and grow as you change and grow. However, you should set a baseline from here, as you just did with the first question. Once again, you will contemplate one of a few general approaches and determine which is applicable to you. Are you practicing for improvement, empowerment, or inquiry?

Those who practice for improvement pursue the work for self-enrichment of a spiritual nature. They wish to become their best selves and move further along the path to a higher state of being. This is what might be considered the highest path, and it is the one most encouraged by this system.

Those who practice for empowerment wish to enact their will on the world around them. They wish to use the art to improve their material situation or mold the world in a way that pleases them. This is not inherently inappropriate, as sometimes physical beings need help paying the rent, but it can quickly become dangerous if abused. If this is your reason, remember that you must enact your will very carefully. Magic that comes from a place of avarice perpetuates a mindset that chains the magician to the suffering of the material world eternally. It is of the utmost importance to remember that the art is to be practiced for good. Do good whenever and wherever you can, and if you cannot find it in you to do good, then at the very least do no harm.

Those who practice for inquiry take the view of *ars gratia artis* (art for art's sake), and they practice through a great desire to discover what secrets and revelations the art of magic holds for them. It could be argued that these practitioners really practice for improvement and do not yet know it. The manifestation of magical curiosity may be an inner desire for transcendental growth expressing itself.

Most practitioners can generally identify one or more of these motivations in themselves. Reflect on your reason for pursuing magic. From where does your will to master the art originate? Take note of your thoughts on this in your tome, and perhaps reflect on whether they change after engaging in the exercises in the first section of this book.

It is important to understand why you are pursuing the great work that is magic. The doors you will open on your journey can be difficult, sometimes nigh impossible, to close. You will be exposed to ideas and entities that can reveal things that may prove transformational to your experience of consciousness. Once you have glimpsed the mechanism of existence, its revolutions will always live behind your eyes. Once you have tasted the nectar of understanding, all other sustenance may be as ash in your mouth. Do not undertake the journey of the sorcerer lightly. Know why you are embarking.

Here is a good place to speak about the notion of establishing a compassionate practice. It is important to understand that magic is something you enact through yourself, and as such, it influences your life in the manner you ordain. This is to say that if you practice with ill intent, you will receive ill intent, and if you practice with beneficence, so too will you enjoy the like. As you progress through these pages, you will encounter notions of the infinite nature of the self and the interconnectedness of all consciousnesses. Through magic your will may be manifest. As you say so, you create. What you create for others, you create for yourself, and the reverse is also true. As such, it is paramount to treat yourself and others with compassion. It is also paramount to understand the principle of self-sovereignty, which states that all sapient creatures are sacred and inviolate as they are the sole enactors of their will. Never should you attempt to enforce your own will upon others through use of the high art of magic.

Such actions end only calamitously. Rather, we magicians should always endeavor to work toward the highest good for all.

As in any exercise of power, the use of the great art of magic demands responsibility in its practice. It would be remiss not to speak of this before proceeding into the illumination of the nature of the eidolons. Magic is not, like electricity, an unfeeling force to be channeled indiscriminately with no will of its own. Magic is of will, and magic is will. It is an art used to tap into a force that permeates all things—a consciousness of its own far beyond singular manifestation. Knowing this, we must also know that magic is beyond hatred. Indeed, as it is inside all things that possess it equally, it is distinctly beneficent toward all things. As such, it is not to be used to destroy or harm any other thing that possesses sentience. In this application, we consider the abrogation of will to be tantamount to harm. Furthermore, magic is to be practiced for the highest good whenever possible. To put it simply, always practice magic for the good of all if you are able. If you cannot and must practice for the good of yourself alone, then it should at the very least do no harm, and you should include infringement upon another person's free will in your definition of harm. Failure to act in good faith will visit negative effects upon you. When you fail to respect the harmony of magic, or you sow discord in your dealings with an eidolon, it will hinder your ability to perform magic reliably in the future.

As magicians, not only are we to operate for the highest good at all times, but we must seek to become comfortable with the uncomfortable and at home in the unknown. We are to bring the Promethean fire of our art to illuminate places where injustice festers. In bettering ourselves, we are able to better the world, and therein all conscious beings are lifted. I communicate these notions to you because I have found that it is too easy for many to become lost in the art, to focus only on their own revelations, and to shrink from the world into which they were incarnated. This is a great loss, for as magicians, we possess faculties that can be brought to bear in powerful acts of kindness. Not everyone is necessarily positioned to make major systemic changes in the world, but certainly we are all capable of random acts of spontaneous and unrestrained kindness.

However, first we must listen for those opportunities with the same attentiveness with which we listen for the whispers of the eidolons.

Similarly, we must choose the circles in which we operate with the same care we exercise in tending our tomes. It is vital that we understand who we allow a seat at our table, for what is dinner to the wolf is death to the rabbit. To fraternize with those who willfully choose to harm others is to be complicit in that harm. It falls upon us to denounce such actions in the hopes of causing change through our dissent. If no change comes from this, then we must exercise our will to remove ourselves from groups and affiliations that violate the principles by which we operate.

Our art also endows us with a great capacity for self-reflection. To ignore this capacity is to practice magic disingenuously. It is vital that we introspect on the harmful patterns we have adopted and do our best to deprogram them. Whether inherited through our own traumas, the expectations of our social groups, or personal biases, we all have ingrained patterns of harm that we must untangle to move forward as magicians and as people. Do not neglect this work.

Chapter 2
ENERGY

All magic is fueled by energy. Whether you believe it is an inner spiritual or psychological energy or an external all-permeating energy is entirely yours for interpretation. How you have approached your paradigm will determine whether you see the exercises ahead as allegorical or literal, but it will not affect their efficacy. Within this system, energy is defined as the well of power from which you draw and shape with your will into being, and the various effects can be described as magic. One of the first concepts you must understand is that all living things contain energy—a raw biological energy, at least—and all sapient things manifest the energy that comprises thought. All mundane worldly actions, from jogging to drawing, require the expenditure of some measure of physical or mental energy. However, to use these energies for the work of magic is personally draining. Magic is extraordinary, and its practice should be energized from an extraordinary source. This brings you to the second concept you must address. Existence itself has energy in an amount that defies human measure, and this is what you may draw from to fuel your magic. Whether you believe this energy to be raw, ambient, physical energy devoid of consciousness, or a divinity that suffuses all things depends upon the paradigm you have defined for yourself. You should take a moment to reflect on energy and record your thoughts in your tome.

Moving forward with the notion that all of existence is permeated with energy of some kind, the next logical question is how you might access it. This question has been answered by many traditions over the millennia with striking parallels. Presented here, you will find two systems that describe energy centers in the body, or the spirit body perhaps, that act as conduits of this universal energy through the human form, which channels our consciousness during our time on earth. In addition, you will be introduced to exercises designed to help you deliberately amplify the flow of this energy and center yourself in its steady emanation.

Two Energy Systems

Here you will find two common traditional energy systems described. You are encouraged to engage in the exercises provided for both following this section, taking notes on each one, until you find the methodology that works best for you. You will be introduced now to the chakra system and Sephiroth (singular: Sephira).

Chakras

The chakra system is a modality for mapping the energy centers of the body. This system has its origin in ancient Tantric practices and exists in several variations throughout Hindu and Buddhist faiths. The version I put forth for you now is the seven-chakra system. The chakra system is thousands of years old and has a rich cultural and religious history beyond the very simple use we employ here. It is my desire to be appreciative of this system, as I was introduced to it, and not appropriative of it, and as such, I will only speak of it in the manner that it has entered the Western occult consciousness. For the purposes of this work, we need only know that chakras are energy centers in the body—wheels of clear light—and they are as follows:

- *Crown chakra:* located at the top of the head; lit in brilliant violet
- *Third eye chakra:* located at the forehead; lit in effulgent indigo

- **Throat chakra:** located at the neck; lit in shining blue
- **Heart chakra:** located in the middle of the chest; lit in radiant green
- **Solar plexus chakra:** located at the base of the rib cage; lit in lustrous gold
- **Sacral chakra:** located just below the belly button; lit in glowing orange
- **Root chakra:** located in the pelvic bowl; lit in smoldering red

The meanings of these chakras, their Sanskrit names, and other ways to work with them can be researched at your leisure and doing so is highly encouraged.

Sephiroth

The Sephiroth are the spheres on the Qabalistic Tree of Life, and they are inextricably woven into the fabric of the Western esoteric tradition. Writings on these energy centers by ceremonial magicians are myriad and are worthy of pursuing. Some Qabalists define eleven Sephiroth, and some define ten, depending on whether they regard the sphere Da'ath as a true Sephira. Here we only concern ourselves with the five spheres of the Middle Pillar of the Tree of Life as they are those with which the coming exercises interact. Those five Sephiroth are as follows:

- **Kether:** located at the top of the head; lit in radiant white
- **Da'ath:** located at the neck; shining in bright silver
- **Tiphareth:** located at the solar plexus; emanating in effulgent gold
- **Yesod:** located in the bowl of the pelvis; pulsating in purest purple
- **Malkuth:** located between the feet when standing straight; shaded in nascent black

Finding Center

In addition to the flow of energy necessary to manifest the work of magic, one must also abide in a certain state of present consciousness. To manifest true affect, you must rid yourself of the static that clings to human consciousness as it wades through the vagaries of material existence. The exercises to follow serve two purposes. The first is to achieve a state of present moment awareness, and the second is to evoke the flow of universal energy through your newly clarified presence. A concept found in both the Tantric tradition, from which the chakra system originates, and the Qabalistic tradition is that of connecting yourself to universal or all-pervading energy. The two, however, define the source and nature of that energy differently. In this practice you have defined, or are defining, that energy for yourself. The following exercises serve to connect you to this source of energy so that you may draw from its infinite abundance to power your craft. They do this through allowing you to find a state of center, an abiding, calm, present-moment consciousness known as *rigpa* in Tibet, which translates to "knowledge of the ground." Ground in this sense refers to a primordial state of consciousness at the root of all things. It finds its counterpart in the Ein Sof of Qabalistic work, which is the all-permeating root consciousness of the unmanifested god before the act of creation.

When we talk about present-moment awareness, we are speaking of a state of existing in the moment without attachment to what has come before or what may follow after. It is a state of feeling without succumbing; it is standing in the river without being taken by the current. It is a state of perceiving without judging, existing as a witness to existence. To assist in achieving this state, it is important to understand, at least on an intellectual level to begin with, that you are not your body or your thoughts. You are consciousness currently occupying a role in the puppet show of physical incarnation. In a state of calm abiding, you are pure perception and as close as you can be to the true essence of being while here in manifest reality.

If you master no other skill in this book but present-moment consciousness, you will have gained something immeasurably valuable. Without this awareness, you are a somnambulist, wading through life as if in a dream. You will eat, sleep, and speak without being fully present for these actions. You will have given up control to your mind, allowing the autopilot function to steer your physical form rather than making deliberate decisions as to the direction of your growth. One may slip in and out of present-moment awareness for years, decades, or even lifetimes before being able to abide in it without interruption, but each time it is experienced, it is infinitely beneficial in paving the way for its sustained mastery.

Being present-aware—living in an eternal moment, understanding that you are a limitless being experiencing the limitation of incarnation but not bound by it—does not end when you rise from seated meditation. It is likely you will come to this realization for the first time in meditation, but it is meant to be perpetual. Whether you are at work, on a bus, or at a party, it does not matter. The positioning of your physical body in space and time is immaterial to your abiding in that moment consciously, whatever it may be.

It is important to make a distinction here between intellectual understanding and true gnosis. To understand with the mind is a beautiful thing, and it is the basis of the myriad arts and sciences which enrich our world. However, when we speak of realizing your infinite nature, we are talking about experiencing it with the totality of your being. It is the difference in understanding between having read a book about a distant land and having visited, tasted its delicacies, taken in its landscape, and immersed yourself in the nuances of its culture. You can say, "I am limitless, only this moment exists, and I reside within it" without actually experiencing it, and the goal is to experience that profound state of abiding.

To help you come to a state of present-moment awareness, three exercises are presented for your use. Two exercises are presented from long-standing traditions, and one novel exercise is offered as well. It is encouraged that you try each one at least once to get a feel for which exercise resonates with you. Each exercise is also followed by a secondary exercise. The secondary exercise is designed to expand your awareness outward once you achieve a foundational sense of center and present-moment awareness. Read through all of the exercises in this chapter to familiarize yourself with them before beginning to practice them. After you try each exercise set for the first time, make note of your observations in your tome. Each following time, you may wish to take note of any changes, feelings, visions, or revelations.

You will now discover the Middle Pillar, which is rooted in Qabalistic work; the Rigpa Meditation, drawing from Tantric practice; and the White Thread Meditation, which serves as a wholly secular counterpart to the prior two ancient traditions.

The Middle Pillar Exercise

The Middle Pillar Exercise was highly regarded by ceremonial magicians of the nineteenth and twentieth century, although its roots reach much further back in history. It is a standing exercise, and it is followed by a counterpart exercise called the Qabalistic Axis, a variant of the more traditional Qabalistic Cross. The versions of these exercises that I have drawn from come from the writings of Israel Regardie.[3] In these exercises, you will be interfacing with a limitless well of cosmic energy, the nature of which you must reflect on and determine for yourself. The terminology used is Abrahamic in nature as this is based upon Judaic mysticism, and the words used are Hebrew. There are a few twists in this version inherited from early Christian mysticism. This first exercise is called the Middle Pillar because it deals with the Sephiroth located in the Middle Pillar of the Qabalistic Tree of Life—the pillar of harmony between the two opposing pillars that represent mercy and severity, expansion and retraction, and growth and decay. Here we find parallels with the seventh-century Buddhist philosopher Shandao's parable of the two rivers and the white path. The white path here is interpreted as the path of harmony between the river of fire and the river of water, which in turn represent aggression and passivity, and we can liken them to severity and mercy.

Before you begin your exercise, make sure you are in a calm and private environment where interruption is unlikely to occur. Ensure there is sufficient space around you that you may extend your arms in all directions without obstruction.

To begin, stand up straight with your shoulders relaxed, feet together, and your arms by your side. Various practitioners recommend you stand facing eastward as this direction holds meaning to several mystery schools

---

3. Regardie, *The Middle Pillar*, 79–109.

and represents dawning, beginnings, and the source of wisdom. If you have a compass or compass application available, feel free to face eastward. However, as the world in which we live is by and large illusory, your intention is more important than the orientation of your transient body.

In a standing position, begin to breathe deeply. Breathe in steadily, hold that breath in your lungs, then breathe out and keep your lungs empty for a moment. Do this at the slowest pace that you find comfortable. Alternatively, you may breathe in deeply and breathe out slowly for about 50 percent longer than you spent breathing in. These meditative rhythmic breath techniques are meant to foster clarity and receptivity respectively. Breathe in this way for one to five minutes, until you feel sufficiently relaxed and free of nervous physical energy.

As you stand and practice your breath exercises, imagine that the world around you fades away and you are surrounded by an infinite field of stars, the ink and the black of space. Abide in this place, weightless and in harmony with the emptiness that is pure potentiality. After a comfortable time residing in this calm, perceive high above you a sphere of pure white light, which is the metaphorical center of all creation, the resonant demiurge of existence. As you continue your rhythmic breathing, draw down a pillar of pure white light from that sphere above you to the crown of your head. Watch it descend until it touches your head. Upon that touch, feel a blazing white sphere, a smaller mirror of the one so far above, ignite upon the crown of your head. This is the Sephira Kether. Before proceeding further, take a few more breaths, each one drawing further light down from the heavens and into the brilliantly charged Kether. Feel it vibrate with pure energy. Having done so, now it is time to charge the first Sephira through incantation. You will need to pronounce each syllable clearly and distinctly, resonating the sound in your diaphragm so that it vibrates through your whole body as much as possible. Incant the word *Ehyeh*, which is pronounced eh-HEE-yay. Do so a minimum of three times, but as many times as you require before you feel that the Sephira Kether is suffused with divine light, before proceeding.

At this point you should be visualizing a column of white light descending from on high to the crown of your head. The next step is to draw down that light in an unbroken pillar through each Sephiroth one by one. Continue your rhythmic breathing, visualizing that light descending further, from Kether at your crown down to your throat, with each breath. When you perceive that the column of light has reached your throat, visualize a brilliant silver sphere blaze into existence. This is the second Sephira, Da'ath. As you breathe, visualize the continuing descent of light from on high, through Kether, filling Da'ath. To charge Da'ath, you will incant with the same vibratory technique introduced for Kether. The incantation for Da'ath is *Yhvh Elohim*, pronounced YEH-hoh-vah el-OH-heem. Do so a minimum of three times, but as many times as you require before you feel that the Sephira Da'ath is suffused with divine light, before proceeding.

Proceeding, you will now continue to draw down the column of white light through the prior Sephiroth and into your solar plexus with each breath. When you feel the column has reached your solar plexus, visualize a sphere of effulgent gold blaze into being. This is the third Sephira, Tiphareth. As you breathe, visualize the continuing descent of light from on high, through the Sephiroth above, filling Tiphareth. To charge Tiphareth, you will incant using the now familiar vibratory technique. The incantation for Tiphareth is *Yhvh Eloah Va Da'ath*, which is pronounced YEH-hoh-vah el-OH-ah vah da-ATH. Do so a minimum of three times, but as many times as you require before you feel that the Sephira Tiphareth is suffused with divine light, before proceeding.

Proceeding once more, you will continue to draw down the column of white light through the prior Sephiroth and into your pelvic bowl with each breath. When you feel the column has reached your pelvic bowl, visualize a sphere of bright purple blaze into being. This is the fourth Sephira of the Middle Pillar, Yesod. As you breathe, visualize the continuing descent of light from on high, through the Sephiroth above, filling Yesod. To charge Yesod, you will incant using the vibratory technique. The incantation for Yesod is *Shaddai El Chai*, which is pronounced sha-DYE EL KYE. Do so a minimum of three times, but as many times as you require before you feel that the Sephira Yesod is suffused with divine light, before proceeding.

Moving toward the completion of the first portion of this exercise, you will continue to draw down the column of white light through the prior Sephiroth and into the space between your feet with each breath. When you feel the column has reached the space between your feet, visualize a sphere of onyx black pulsate into being. This is the fifth Sephira of the Middle Pillar, Malkuth. As you breathe, visualize the continuing descent of light from on high, through the Sephiroth above, filling Malkuth. To charge Malkuth, you will incant using the vibratory technique. The incantation for Malkuth is *Adonai Ha Aretz*, which is pronounced ah-DOH-nye HA AH-rets. Do so a minimum of three times, but as many times as you require before you feel that the Sephira Malkuth is suffused with divine light, before proceeding.

Now the brilliant light of existence has descended through you and is held in your energy system. The exercise is almost complete, but not quite. Continuing to breathe rhythmically, visualize and feel that column of divine energy descend from Malkuth through the ground, through the rock and soil of the earth's crust, through the caves and past the fossils, into the center of the earth. Here, visualize an immense sphere of white light tinged with green, mirroring the light so far above. Contact that white-green energy, and as you breathe, draw it up the column and into yourself, moving up each Sephiroth until it resides in your crown and charges your entire body. You may then proceed to visualize this energy moving in patterns throughout your being, rising from the earth through each Sephira to Kether, and then descending through your left side, and then flowing back up to Kether through your right side. Alternatively, you may visualize it rising like the two serpents of the caduceus around your body to Kether and, from Kether, endlessly pouring out like water over the entirety of your being. Abide in whichever flow you choose for a time. When you feel ready, take three deep breaths and visualize the world around you slowly fading into being, the infinite star-scape fading away. Acknowledge the flow remains, even after the exercise is complete. A phrase or action to signify the end of work is helpful to set an endpoint from which you may step again into the mindset of daily life. You may find your own, but for now, simply say, "So it is."

What you have accomplished here is establishing a flow of energy from which you may draw the great power needed for the successful application of the work of magic. You are bringing energy down from the source of all things, directing it through yourself as a conduit to the earth upon which you reside, and drawing it back up in that stable form to apply as you see fit. This—or one of the similar exercises that accomplish the same end, which you will find later in this chapter—should be practiced regularly. For the first month you familiarize yourself with this flow, it is recommended you practice daily. After that time, daily practice is still recommended but several times weekly may suffice as life's other obligations arise.

Adding the Qabalistic Axis

After your first several times completing the Middle Pillar Exercise, you will be ready to add on the Qabalistic Axis, and the purpose of this is to expand your newly centered awareness outward and open yourself to the flow of energies beyond.

After completing the Middle Pillar, but before ending the exercise, raise your dominant hand to your forehead and intone, using the resonant voice you should now have become accustomed to, the word *Ateh*, pronounced ah-TAY. Visualize the brilliant section of the column of light that runs from Tiphareth up to the divine sphere blaze even brighter. Next, bring your hand to the center of your chest, and intone the word *Malkuth*, pronounced mal-KOOTH. Visualize the section of the column of light running from Tiphareth down to the earth center blaze even brighter. Next, bring your hand to the shoulder opposite your dominant hand, and intone the phrase *Ve Geburah*, pronounced VAY geh-BOO-rah. Visualize a new column of light blaze into existence, extending from the middle of your chest out through your nondominant shoulder and into eternity. Now, bring your hand to your dominant shoulder, and intone the phrase *Ve Gedulah*, pronounced VAY geh-DOO-lah. Visualize a new column of light blaze into existence, extending from the middle of your chest out through your dominant shoulder and into eternity, connecting to the pillar extending from your other shoulder and joining into one, revealing a cruciform shape of two pillars intersecting through the center of your chest. The middle pillar and this new horizon pillar are formed from the right and left. Next, bring your hand to the center of your chest where the two pillars intersect, and intone the phrase *La Olam*, pronounced LAH oh-LAHM. Visualize another pillar blaze into existence, expanding ever backward in a straight line from the center of your chest. Keep your hand centered, and intone *Amen*, pronounced AH-men. Visualize the central pillar created when intoning *La Olam* now extending through you and out the front of your chest, expanding ever forward. Continue your rhythmic breathing, and feel your awareness dance along these three pillars: the x, y, and z axes of existence. When you feel sufficiently calm and aware, end your Middle Pillar Exercise as described in the prior section.

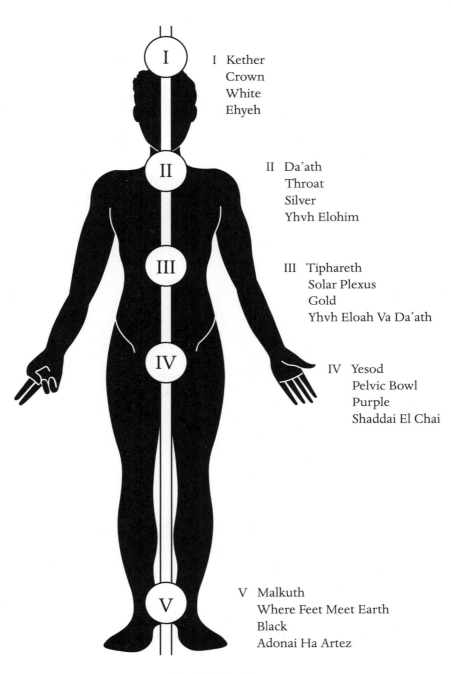

I   Kether
    Crown
    White
    Ehyeh

II Da'ath
    Throat
    Silver
    Yhvh Elohim

III Tiphareth
    Solar Plexus
    Gold
    Yhvh Eloah Va Da'ath

IV Yesod
    Pelvic Bowl
    Purple
    Shaddai El Chai

V   Malkuth
    Where Feet Meet Earth
    Black
    Adonai Ha Artez

Middle Pillar Diagram

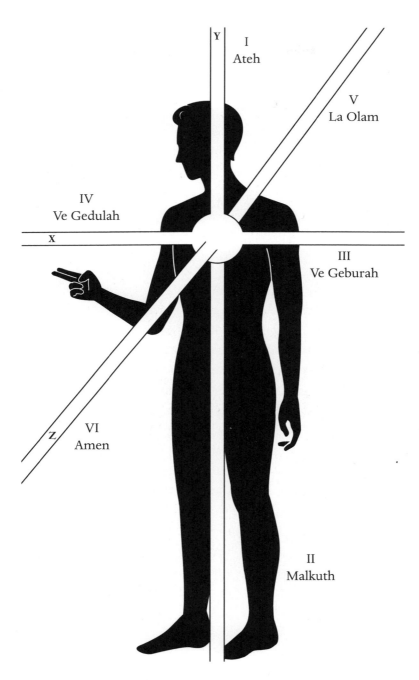

I
Ateh

V
La Olam

IV
Ve Gedulah

X

III
Ve Geburah

VI
Amen

Z

Y

II
Malkuth

Qabalistic Axis Diagram

The Rigpa Meditation

The Rigpa Meditation has many parallels with the Middle Pillar but originates in a different tradition. This version of the Rigpa Meditation is put together from an amalgamation of chakra alignment exercises I have been exposed to over the course of my life. *Rigpa* is a Tibetan word that translates literally to "knowledge of the ground" or "awareness," but philosophically it refers to a state of interconnected and all-aware mind. Rigpa as a concept is beautifully presented in the Dzogchen school of Buddhism. I am not, and would not presume to speak as, an expert on Buddhism, but I would encourage reading into Dzogchen literature as an addition to your meditative toolbox and to gain a depth of knowledge on this concept I am attempting to respectfully touch on here. This Rigpa Meditation eschews the need for several incantations, favoring instead the single sacred syllable *Om*.

As in the Middle Pillar, this technique begins with breathing. The same rhythmic breath techniques as described earlier, with which you should now be familiar, should be applied. You will again be drawing energy down from the infinite source of all things, visualized as high above your head, and through your energy centers into the earth and back up into your being. The differences are in the position of your body, the energy center system used, and the intonations for both charging the centers and ending the exercise.

You will begin the Rigpa Meditation by sitting cross-legged on the ground or a comfortable cushion with your spine straight, head up, and your hands on your knees or in your lap. Begin your rhythmic breathing technique, focusing simply on your breath until you feel calm and aware of your own awareness. Visualize the world around you fading away, replaced with an infinite expanse of twinkling stars. Above you, perceive the paradoxical center of infinity, a great bright light that vibrates in a high, clear tone. As you breathe, visualize its light descending toward the crown chakra.

Upon reaching your crown chakra, feel the light suffuse it and cause it to bloom like a many petaled violet lotus. Feel it become clear, clean, and bright. After a few breaths of taking in this feeling, you will charge your crown chakra by intoning the syllable *Om* in a resonant tone a minimum of three times. Dwell in a feeling of bliss here for a few moments, basking in a clear feeling of illumination.

As you have already gone through the Middle Pillar, you are familiar with the pattern established. For each chakra below the crown, you will draw down the clear light of existence and charge that chakra, visualized as a spinning wheel of energy, with the syllable *Om*, as described.

Through your crown chakra, draw down cascading light to your third eye chakra, located at your forehead. Feel your third eye chakra rouse and begin to vibrate, to spin like a gyroscope as it shines with indigo light flowing from the heavens, through the chakra above and into its essence. Intone the syllable *Om* three times at a steady pace, feeling the light in your third eye chakra intensify with each intonation. Dwell in this feeling for several breaths before shifting your awareness downward into your throat chakra.

As the light flows downward, like a pure, clear waterfall, feel it come to reside in your throat chakra. As the light enters your throat chakra, feel it dance with radiant blue light, spinning like a moon in orbit. As you feel the light charge and expand your throat chakra, again intone *Om* three times at a steady pace. With each intonation, feel the clear light refresh you. Dwell in this clear feeling for several breaths before once again shifting your awareness to your next chakra, the heart chakra in the middle of your chest.

Through the chakras above, again you will draw down the clear light of existence. This time you will draw it into your heart. As the clear light enters your heart chakra, feel it blossom in a verdant green, the scent of the forest accompanying it. Feel it spin like the earth, emanating compassion for all living things. Breathe deeply, and steadily intone *Om* three times. Dwell in a feeling of oneness with other living creatures for a moment before shifting your awareness to your next chakra, at your solar plexus.

As you draw down the light of existence through the chakras above, it comes to reside now in your solar plexus, illuminating it a brilliant gold. Feel the pulsating centrifugal energy here, at the core of your physical form. Reside in awareness of it for a moment, and feel an energizing tide of light wash over you. Intone *Om* again, three times as before, and dwell in this energizing tide before moving forward. Again, focus your awareness downward, to your sacral chakra below your belly button.

As the multitiered waterfall of light flows down through each chakra above it, feel it enter your sacral chakra. As it touches upon it, envision a deep orange light, and feel a calm joy enter you. Feel a whirlpool of contented warmth as the light swirls, and again breathe deeply, slowly intoning *Om* three times. Once more you will direct your awareness and the light that will follow it downward to your next chakra, the root chakra in your pelvic bowl.

As the pure light of existence enters the final focal point of this energy system, having passed through all above it, feel your root chakra shine in a ruby effulgence. Allow a feeling of great health and comfort to arise as your root chakra spins with gyroscopic light. Breathe slowly as you again intone *Om* three times before envisioning the light flowing downward again, out of your body and into the earth.

Visualize the divine light of existence permeating through the earth and arriving at its center. There it will meet a great white-green sphere of earthly energy. That earthly energy will flow up to your root chakra, and it will ascend to each chakra in turn to arrive at your crown and flow down again like falling petals, suffusing your whole being. You will abide in that flow until you are ready to arise, watching the world fade back into existence and ending your exercise with a deep breath and slow exhale.

This is the second exercise used to establish and maintain a state of centered energy flow and present-moment consciousness. You should practice it along with the Middle Pillar and consider the two interchangeable.

Adding the Net of Pearls Meditation

As the Qabalistic Axis is the counterpart to the Middle Pillar, the Net of Pearls Meditation is the counterpart to the Rigpa Meditation. It is named as such due to a Vedic concept that states, to paraphrase, that the heavens of the god Indra are an infinite net of pearls, each one reflected in the other.[4] In this visualization, each pearl orb is a universe in the cosmic multiverse, and all are connected by threads of light along each axis.

When your Rigpa Meditation is complete, but before you transition into material consciousness, bring your attention to the glowing green wheel of your heart chakra. As you begin to do so, picture yourself expanding outward

---

4. Odin, *Process Metaphysics and Hua-Yen Buddhism*, 16–17.

as your heart chakra glows brighter until you yourself are a cosmos—a universe in yourself. Now intone the syllable *Om*. As you do so, visualize lines of light expanding from you to the front and back, right and left, and above and below. These lines eventually contact other spheres of light. Hold your awareness on these spheres, and again intone *Om*. Now envision lines of light go forth from all these other spheres you have touched, each touching new spheres beyond them, cascading into an infinite grid with a sphere at each axis. For a final time, intone *Om*, and see all the spheres blaze with clear light. Now abide in this expanded awareness for a time. Stay until you again draw yourself inward, focusing on your own universe, your own column of light from the ineffable center of infinity to the earth. From here, close your meditation as you did the Rigpa Meditation, with the fading in of the material world and a slow exhalation.

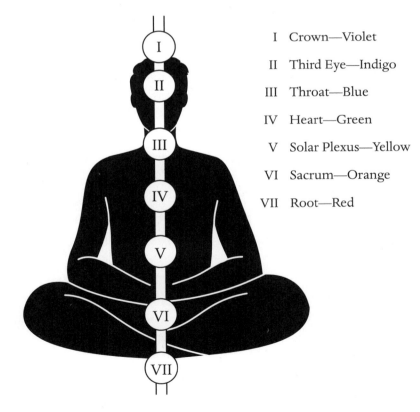

I	Crown—Violet
II	Third Eye—Indigo
III	Throat—Blue
IV	Heart—Green
V	Solar Plexus—Yellow
VI	Sacrum—Orange
VII	Root—Red

Rigpa Meditation Diagram

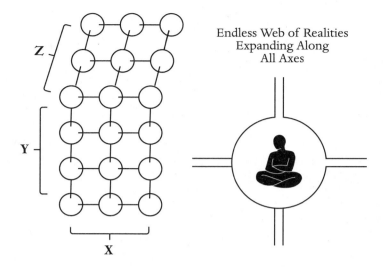

Net of Pearls Meditation Diagram

A Secular Alternative: The White Thread Meditation

The White Thread Meditation is presented as an entirely secular alternative to the previous two exercises. It is an invention of my own rather than a spiritual centering technique from an ancient lineage. While the practices in this book are considered syncretic, an amalgamation of exercises and traditions that seek after the same mysteries, there is space to acknowledge and respect that all people have varying comfort levels with assorted spiritual traditions.

This meditation can be completed while standing or sitting. All that matters is that the position can be maintained comfortably. In this meditation, you will not interact with imagery of divinity or universality and will instead engage with your own consciousness.

As you stand or sit, you will begin the rhythmic breathing techniques discussed in the first exercise. Do so until you have reached a calm, aware state. Now visualize yourself sinking into yourself, entering an infinite space that exists in your own mind. Above you, visualize a brilliant sphere of light. This represents your inner potential, or higher self. Far below you, envision a green sphere of light. This represents your connection to the world around you, your senses, your emotions, and other ways in which you interact with the physical world.

As you continue your rhythmic breathing, envision a white thread of light descending from the sphere above until it hangs in front of you. When you perceive it as hanging at the level of your chest, envision yourself taking hold of it and floating down slowly to sit atop the green sphere. When you are atop the green sphere, touch the white thread to it, and watch as it attaches itself and golden light begins to pulsate across it, moving back and forth between the green and white spheres. Envision yourself holding on to the now taut white thread, and feel the golden energy flow through you like a warming electricity. As you experience this sensation, resonantly intone the word *Aura*, pronounced AWE-rah. This is a word chosen to vibrate within your chest easily and not for any other connotations or meanings invested in it, which are not part of this exercise. After you have intoned this phrase a minimum of nine times, abide in this state while rhythmically breathing until you feel ready to bring your awareness back to your physical body rather than your mental one. Mark this transition with the phrase "So it is." Understand that this connection between your everyday self and your inner potential is still established as you go about your day.

Adding the Weaving Meditation

Like the traditional exercises detailed earlier, the White Thread Meditation has an additional step to incorporate once you are comfortable with the initial work. This expanding practice is called the Weaving Meditation.

When you deem your White Thread Meditation complete, but before you rouse yourself from it, visualize a golden tapestry beginning to weave itself from just below the green sphere on which you sit, expanding in all directions. This tapestry reflects the light of the white sphere above you and is intricately patterned. Depending on the angle from which you view it, you may see a chronicle of all life on earth being drawn, an intricate and expanding fractal, or a complex series of equations being written. As you watch this tapestry expand ever outward, expanding your awareness with it, intone the word *Sophos*, pronounced SO-fos, which means wisdom. Abide here for a time, taking in the infinite weaving of the tapestry, until you feel fit to rouse yourself and end the meditation as normal.

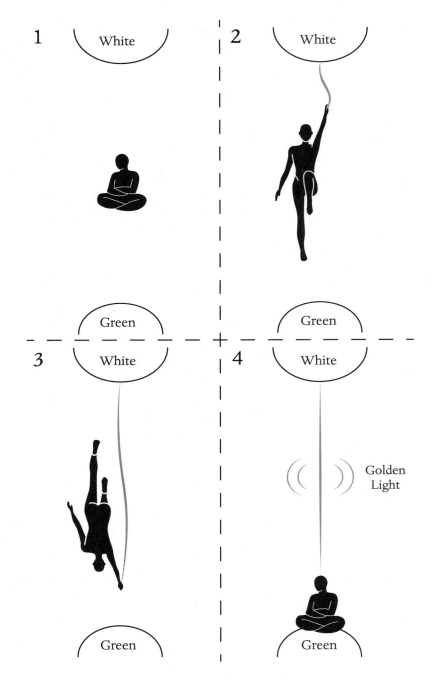

White Thread Meditation Diagram

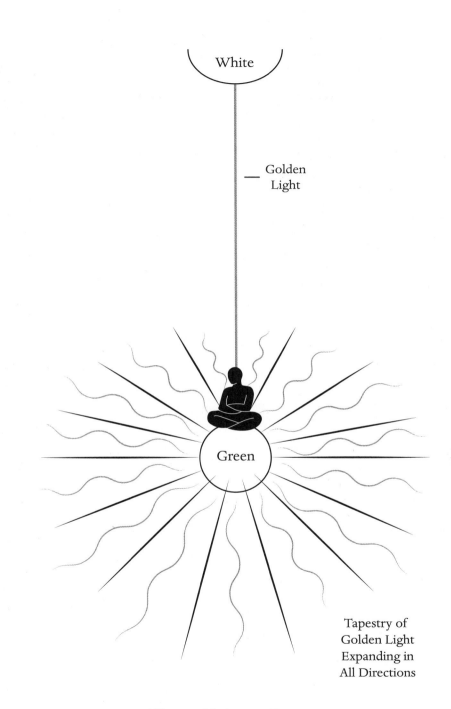

White

Golden
Light

Green

Tapestry of
Golden Light
Expanding in
All Directions

Weaving Meditation Diagram

Recording Your Journey

Now you have engaged in three centering and expanding exercise sets and made your observations of each in your working book. It is important that you incorporate one of these exercises into your daily routine as often as possible. Engaging in these practices will help to foster a state of consciousness conducive to the practice of the art of magic. In addition, they will tune your senses to facets of existence that our daily mundane lives do not encourage us to comprehend. Most notably, in this system, these exercises are the very beginning of learning to listen for the subtle whispers of the eidolons. It is advised that you practice at least once a day for several weeks before proceeding to the exercises to follow. Try each of the exercises at least once to see which you feel most connected to. You can choose to focus on that one or switch between them with no detriment to your progress. Having a steady conduit of energy is necessary to perform the following work without experiencing fatigue through the expenditure of your own.

Chapter 3
CALLING THE
QUARTERS

———————◦———————

Now that you have begun to establish a magical practice with your daily meditations, jotting down observations of note in your tome, you are prepared to extend the workings of your magic beyond yourself. In the meditations outlined earlier, you drew from existence to expand your own energy and consciousness, and now you will use that flowing conduit you have established to work upon the space around you. This step is the prerequisite to the work that will follow later, in which you will contact and engage with eidolons of varying natures. In order to make that contact, you must have a space defined around you, a locus of control through which no harm may pass to you. This is most often done through a modality generally summarized by the phrase "calling the quarters." It is called this because it is built around the idea of invoking the powers of the four cardinal directions and the entities and elements associated with them. This is done to represent the totality of space and time and all facets and corners of existence. Here you will be introduced to the Lesser Banishing Ritual of the Pentagram, which uses Qabalistic terminology and calls upon the archangels of the cardinal directions. You will also be introduced to the Invocation of the Elementals, which calls upon the elemental rulers. You will also learn a third option, called the Four Vistas Exercise, which focuses on protection through the visualization of impassable terrain.

The Lesser Banishing Ritual of the Pentagram

The Lesser Banishing Ritual of the Pentagram is the counterpart to the Middle Pillar, and it is recommended you perform both the Middle Pillar and the Qabalistic Axis immediately before engaging in this ritual. The Lesser Banishing Ritual of the Pentagram is called such because it banishes all negativity or ill will from the area so you may enact your work within. This exercise comes to us from the Hermetic Order of the Golden Dawn through the writings of Israel Regardie.[5]

You will begin standing, facing east if possible, but again, setting your intention is what matters above all other parameters. As you gaze in front of you, raise your dominant hand with your index and middle fingers pointed outward and your pinkie and ring fingers touching your thumb. This is a position known as the *prana mudra* in yoga. As you will have just completed the Middle Pillar, draw up universal energy and feel it flow from your chest down your dominant arm into the raised fingers of your hand. See this energy flow from your fingertips in white, blue, and purple fire as you draw a five-pointed star, beginning at the bottom left point. When you are finished, visualize this pentagram flaming before you before thrusting your hand into its center and intoning *Yhvh*, the pronunciation of which you learned in chapter 2. Hold this position for a moment, feeling the word flow down your arm and into the pentagram. Then, with your arm still outstretched, turn ninety degrees to face your right. As you do so, envision a line of light moving from the center of the pentagram, making a quarter circle.

Now repeat the process of tracing another pentagram, its center overlapping the line of light you have just brought from the prior pentagram. This time when you complete the pentagram, thrust your fingers into the center where the line of light resides, and intone *Adonai*, another word you have been made familiar with in chapter 2. Hold again, feeling this

---

5. Regardie, *The Middle Pillar*, 79–109.

word resonate down your arm and into the pentagram, before continuing the line of light by turning to your right again, putting your back now to the original pentagram.

Repeat, again, the tracing of the next pentagram, watching it blaze before you. This time as you thrust your hand into the center of the pentagram, intone *Ehyeh*. Again, feel the word vibrate through you and down your arm to the center of the pentagram. Again, you will make a turn to your right, continuing the line of light from the center of the previous pentagram so that you now have ¾ of a circle.

Trace the final pentagram in blue and purple fire before thrusting forth your hand and intoning AGLA, which is representative of the phrase *Ateh Gebur Le Olam Adonai* but which you can vibrate in short form by pronouncing ah-GAY-lah. Again, you will feel the word vibrate down your arm and into the pentagram. Make your final turn to your right, taking the line of light along with you. This action will complete the circle of light, and you will now face the first pentagram. You will remain facing the first pentagram for the rest of this ritual.

Next you will call upon the archangels of the directions and elements. Make sure you are speaking clearly, confidently, and with purpose.

First focus your attention on the pentagram before you and state:

"Before me, Raphael, and your elements of air."

Next you will turn your attention, but not your body, to the pentagram behind you and state:

"Behind me, Gabriel, and your elements of water."

Refocus your attention to the pentagram on your right and state:

"At my right hand, Michael, and your elements of fire."

Now turn your attention to the pentagram to your left and state:

"At my left hand, Uriel, and your elements of earth."

At this point, you may think that you are done with directions but remember that there are three axes of the Qabalistic Axis. As such, we will be calling upon the angelic rulers of Kether and Malkuth, the Sephiroth found at the zenith and nadir of the Middle Pillar, Metatron and Sandalphon. We will associate them with the elements of light and darkness. In this exercise, light is taken to mean closeness to the source of creation, and darkness is taken to mean closeness to material existence. While the Lesser Banishing Ritual of the Pentagram exists in many versions, few practitioners seem to incorporate sentinels at the top and bottom of the ritual sphere. I have always found the practice to be beneficial, but as always, your rituals are yours to edit at your will. Of other notable magicians, Damien Echols, in his work *High Magick*, also incorporates these angelic rulers of Kether and Malkuth into his Lesser Banishing Ritual of the Pentagram.[6]

Continuing, turn your attention above you to the sphere of light that resides there, and state:

"At my crown, Metatron, and your elements of light."

Then turn your attention to the white-green sphere below you and state:

"At my foundation, Sandalphon, and your elements of darkness."

We will also acknowledge the intersection of the axes, or the solar plexus of the practitioner. This intersectional acknowledgment is associated with the element of life, which is the medium through which eternal consciousness interfaces with the material world. When invoking the element of life, I have chosen Yeshua, the Christ figure. However, if that does not work for your practice, you can just as easily invoke another divinity to which you feel close, or simply eschew any name and invoke only the elements of life.

Turn your attention to the Sephira Tiphareth, shining in your solar plexus, and state:

"Within me, Yeshua, and your elements of life."

---

6. Echols, *High Magick*, 97–98.

These preceding axes and directions comprise the cardinal points. However, you may wish to add a final point that is a nod to the boundary line, the liminal state between your circle and material reality. If this appeals to you, focus your attention on the space beyond the circle itself and state:

"Beyond me, Azrael, and your elements of death."

Here we acknowledge that death is what lies beyond the perception of the mortal gaze, and we pay respect to that knowledge.

Your next task is to affirm your borders. Visualize the pentagrams that hang in the air at each cardinal direction and the white circle that joins them through their centers. Speak clearly when you state:

"Four around me flame the pentagrams."

Visualize a final star, a unicursal hexagram that shines from your chest, and state:

"Upon me shines the six-rayed star."

Finally, some practitioners prefer to raise their hands and envision the circle becoming a white dome before lowering them and envisioning that dome becoming a sphere. The symbolism of the directions implies that all foreseeable entry is barred save that which you will, so you may not find it personally beneficial to envision a sphere. This detail is a matter of preference.

Now your circle is ready for the practice of the art. Later on you will receive exercises to engage in when you have established your circle, but for now it is a good time to simply abide in a ritual consciousness or develop your visualizations of the various archangels. When you are ready to leave the circle, you should perform the Qabalistic Axis for a final time and end by shifting your focus from your work and letting your awareness fade back into mundane headspace, ending with the capstone phrase:

"So it is."

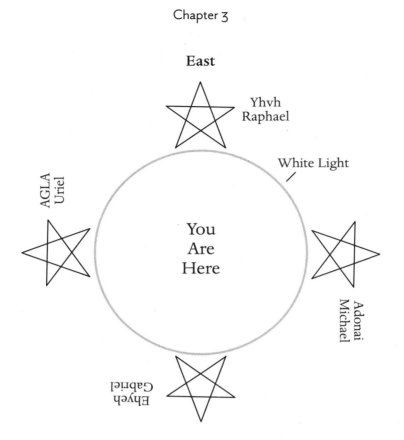

East

Yhvh
Raphael

White Light

AGLA
Uriel

You
Are
Here

Adonai
Michael

Ehyeh
Gabriel

Lesser Banishing Ritual of the Pentagram Diagram

After your first experience with the Lesser Banishing Ritual of the Pentagram, which is often abbreviated as the LBRP, make note of the visualizations, emotions, and ideas that came to you while performing it in your tome. Each time you perform the ritual, until such a time as it has become exceedingly familiar to you, you should make note of any observations you may have. Even after you have become well versed in its practice, you may come across new realizations that warrant recording.

Invocation of the Elementals

While the Lesser Banishing Ritual of the Pentagram evokes Judeo-Christian imagery, the Invocation of the Elementals seeks to accomplish the same space setting with the imagery of elemental spirits. It is practiced very similarly; it simply replaces the pentagrams with the four elemental triangles and the archangels with the elemental rulers. This ritual exists in many forms throughout modern magic and is often found in Wiccan practice.

As before, you will begin by centering yourself with one of the exercises discussed previously: the Middle Pillar, the Rigpa Meditation, or the White Thread Meditation. Having done so, you will rise if you are seated, and face the east if it is discernible. Once again, feel the flow of energy down from eternity, through you to the grounding earth, and back into your being. Again, you will be positioning your dominant hand into the prana mudra. Feel the pure, unfettered, and universal energy flow down your arm and through your fingers.

You will begin by envisioning yellow fog flowing from your fingertips, which you will use to draw an equilateral triangle facing upward, placing a single horizontal line through its center. This is the triangle representative of the element of air. Thrust your hand into its center and, making a turn to face your right, trace a white line that will form the first quarter circle. If you are upholding directionality, you will be facing the south in this position.

From your new position, again draw up from the infinite well of energy, and feel it flow down your arm and into your dominant hand. This time you will be drawing forth deep red flame. With that flame, draw another equilateral triangle. It should face upward with no line through it. This is the elemental triangle of fire. Thrust your hand into its center as you did the previous triangle, and continue the line of light as you make a turn to your right to face the west.

From the west, again call forth the connection to eternity you have forged. Bring its effulgent energy down through your arm and out from your fingertips in a sapphire blue water. Scribe upon the air before you another equilateral triangle; this one should point downward. This is the elemental triangle of water. Thrust your hand into the center of the triangle, and make your third turn to face your right, now to the north, bringing with you the line of light from the center of the triangle.

Now you face the final cardinal direction of this ritual, the north. Here you will, for the final time, call up the inviolable energy of existence and feel it flow through your arm into your dominant hand, focusing itself at your fingertips. For the final triangle, you will be drawing, in verdant emerald vines, an equilateral triangle facing downward with a horizontal line through it. This is the elemental triangle of earth. Thrust your hand to its center, and turn for the final time to your right to again face the east. Bring with you the line of light, completing its circumscription and forming the white circle of your space. You now stand in a circle of white light with four elemental triangles around you.

For your invocations here, you will be calling the four elemental rulers. These spirits, or metaphors, if your paradigm prefers, have been attributed many names by many diverse practitioners. I use the following names as they were those I was taught when first exposed to this rite, and they were presented to me then as traditional names for the elemental rulers. You could also use the names of your preferred elemental divinities or powerful elemental creatures.

Continuing to face the east, speak in a clear, purposeful voice the following invocations:

> *"Attend me, Paralda, ruler of the east quarter, lord of sylphs, and master of air."*
> *"Attend me, Jann, ruler of the south quarter, lord of salamanders, and master of fire."*
> *"Attend me, Niksa, ruler of the west quarter, lord of undines, and master of water."*
> *"Attend me, Gohm, ruler of the north quarter, lord of dryads, and master of earth."*

Note that these elemental spirits are amorphic in form and as genderless as one might expect fire or water to be, and as such, *lord* is merely an honorific that can be considered interchangeable with other honorifics, such as *lady, duke, duchess, king,* or *queen.*

Just as in the Lesser Banishing Ritual of the Pentagram, you may wish to invoke guardians at your crown and foundation. We use the terms *crown* and *foundation* because *above* and *below* hold different occult connotations. As there are no traditional elemental rulers of up and down, you can add the following invocations if you feel they suit your practice:

"Attend me, memories of my ancestors, and be the foundation of my circle."
"Attend me, blessings of my guardians, and crown my circle."

For the final part of the establishment of your circle, you will root yourself in its center and, having called the rulers, evoke their protection. Stand and visualize the elements unifying within yourself. Perhaps roots extend from your feet, ice crystallizes around your legs, wind whips around your torso, and fire dances on your arms. You will develop preferred visualizations as you continue to practice this ritual.

After abiding for a few moments in your visualization, seal the space with the following incantation:

"Oh, rulers of the quarters, lords of the elements, hear me. I consecrate this space for the pursuit of my high art. Let no harm come here. Empower my work that it may be an instrument of good and abide with me here until my purpose is done."

Now is a time to sit and abide with the elements, visualize their rulers in your mind, and otherwise meditate. When you are finished, you may wish to perform one of the expanding meditations you have been taught. When you are ready to end your ritual, thank the elemental rulers, and bid they go in peace. Thank your guardians and ancestors for joining in your work, and bid they watch over you as you traverse existence. Finally, allow the sanctuary to fade from your mind's eye and nonritual awareness to arise again, ending with the capstone phrase:

"So it is."

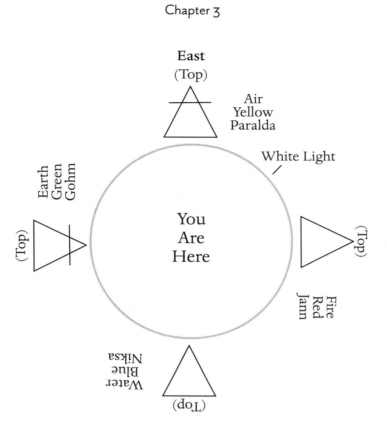

Invocation of the Elementals Diagram

Having completed this second space-defining exercise, it should come as no surprise that I recommend you make notes in your working book. Note how you felt, what ideas or notions came to you, and what visualizations you may have employed. Now that you have engaged in two such exercises, did you find your experiences differed? Do you have a preference already? Make your notes and expand upon them as you familiarize yourself with these two methodologies.

The Four Vistas Exercise

The Four Vistas Exercise is not meant to stand alongside the prior two space-setting exercises. Rather it is an alternative for situations where the above two are simply unfeasible. The efficacy of the Four Vistas Exercise improves exponentially the more experience you have enacting the Lesser Banishing Ritual of the Pentagram and the Invocation of the Elementals. This is due to the fact that the more fully you master the subtle patterns of the work, the easier it will be to use a short form exercise such as this. When one finds the need to consecrate and ward their immediate vicinity of personal space but cannot perform a ritual aloud or move around freely, the Four Vistas Exercise is the shortcut. For instance, if you feel the need to quickly contact an eidolon while on the bus, the Four Vistas Exercise is a better choice than doing so with no sanctum defined at all.

Posture and directionality are immaterial in this exercise. Your first step is to envision your grounding and centering exercise. This is a version without intonation or movements. It is simply visualization of the infinite energy center of the universe flowing into you, through each of your energy centers, into the earth, and back up into your being. Accompany this with slow, relaxed breathing.

Following this, you are to envision yourself in your mind's eye, in whatever position you currently find yourself, atop an impossibly tall pillar of silver-gray stone. Directing your inner vision to the metaphorical east from this pillar, you will see a landscape covered in dense fog and swirling leaves in eddies of wind. Hilltops and trees barely crest above the swirling fog. Above this foggy scene you should envision archangel Raphael, or the elemental ruler Paralda, hovering in quiescent vigilance. When you view this vista, feel the wind upon your body.

Next turn your inner gaze to the south to survey another vista. This one is an endless magma field with dancing flames upon molten stone. Feel the blast of heat from this vista as you look upon it and see the archangel Michael, or the elemental ruler Jann, floating over the heat haze from the peak of a smoldering volcano. When you view this vista, feel heat rise around you and envision the dancing of flames.

Again, turning your inner gaze, look to the west and envision an endless ocean. Waves crash and whirlpools form. Whales crest the surface. Upon this primordial Devonian sea, see that the archangel Gabriel, or elemental ruler Niksa, stands upon the surface of the water. Feel the spray of the sea upon you as you drink in this third vista.

Finally, direct your inner gaze to the north, where a range of mountains rises, studded with precious gems and metals, from a dense and ancient forest. At the peak of the tallest mountain sits the archangel Uriel, or the elemental ruler Gohm, in contemplation. Feel the solid stone beneath you and experience the scent of moss or loam as you contact this final vista.

Understand that vigilant guides protect you from all directions and proceed with your work. This is the quickest and most inconspicuous way to define space when calling eidolons in daily life, and as such, you will become familiar with it quickly and likely tailor its visualizations to suit your preference. Make note of your own technique in your tome as it grows and evolves.

Having completed the first section of this book, you have learned to achieve a calm abiding state and to set your space around you. These are far and away the most crucial elements of a successful magical practice in this system. In addition, you have been directed to take copious notes, which serves as the single most helpful practice for measuring progress and fostering reflection on your journey as a magician. This focus on reflection and notation also serves to prime you for working with eidolons, which will involve recording their details in your tome and developing various ciphers and sigils for the work.

In this chapter, you have been introduced to the foundational elements of the practice of ritual magic in general. These practices are the cornerstone from which you may build the temple of your practice. Do not neglect them. Like any edifice, if erected without a solid foundation, your practice will crumble. It is recommended that you practice one of the centering exercises in the first section of this book regularly for at least thirty days before proceeding forward to the next group of techniques. You can always read ahead, but refrain from engaging in new exercises until you have mastered the foundational elements.

Chapter 4
PREPARING FOR CONTACT

Having learned to center your awareness, you will now be introduced to concepts unique to this system. This section will instruct you on the tools used for the undertakings to be presented in the next chapter and will culminate in a ritual designed as a self-initiatory declaration—a statement of intention to proceed forward in dedication to the work.

In the rituals to follow, you will be utilizing a tool called a scepter. Larger than a wand and shorter than a staff, a scepter is an archetypal symbol of authority and direction of intention. The scepter is divided into two classifications: the scepter of art and the scepter of artifice. The scepter of art is a construct of pure will and is the only true need for the rituals to follow. The scepter of artifice is the physical tool that will represent your scepter of art. It will be an anchor for it on the physical plane, just as your body is the anchor here for your consciousness.

You will also be introduced to the concept of anointing a tool with oil to consecrate and sanctify it, and you will be given the recipe for an anointing oil. Finally, you will learn to use ciphers or symbolic alphabets to codify your writing. These ciphers are recommended for writing down the names of the eidolons you contact so that you may keep them secret. The impetus for this behavior will be discussed further on.

A Note on Tools

It cannot be stressed enough that no tools are strictly necessary. Will is the sole agent that is necessary to operate upon existence. However, as in all things, tools can make a task easier. You can dig a hole with your hands, but a shovel still makes the experience go much more smoothly. There will likely come a time when you have exercised your will so thoroughly through these practices that tools will become wholly unnecessary. That is not to say that you may not still use them. Some practitioners find the creation and use of tools to be rewarding and enriching even after they have moved beyond the point of those tools making any tangible difference to their practice.

This distinction is made to encourage you to withdraw from the notion that the possession of impressive accessories lends any legitimacy to one's practice. Too often, as is the case with much of the tendency to focus on the material world, this thinking is a trap. It is another form of ego accumulation that must be eschewed. How much currency you pour into the procurement of physical trappings does not in any way correlate with how deeply you have internalized your practice. Magic is not a pursuit that is any way affected by economic purchasing power because it interfaces with existence beyond this physical illusion.

The Scepter of Art

The scepter of art requires no physical reagents; it is a construct of pure and unfettered will. When creating this construct, you must begin by calling the quarters in whichever method you prefer, either selected from the space-defining rituals in the first section of this book or developed on your own, taking special attention to be clear and concise in your speech. Upon standing in your completed sanctum, facing the direction at which you began, you must begin to gather energy. Several months of practice should have by this time expanded your ability to serve as an energetic conduit. Begin to draw energy down from eternity, up through the earth, and into your being, maintaining your rhythmic breathing through this process. When you feel you have gathered a great well of energy, direct its flow down your arms and stretch your hands out before you, palms facing one another. Envision energy flowing from your hands and meeting between them, forming into a thin cylinder the length of your arm that begins to glow as a rod of pure light. Energy should be flowing continuously up through you and into this rod, your nascent scepter.

From here, you are in an uncharted country, for each magician's scepter is unique to them. Begin to visualize what energies it manifests, what shape it takes, and what it is called, if you wish to name it. Is it a caduceus entwined with serpents of light? Is it a winged shepherd's crook? Perhaps an octagonal amethyst bar covered in gilded eyes? There is no limit to your scepter of art because it is made of your will. Abide in its design, making it appear as you so wish. Do not worry about getting it "right." You may remake or edit this scepter at any time by repeating this ritual.

When you have formed your scepter of art as you see fit, feel it drift into your dominant hand and hold it before you. Abide in its presence for a time, and when you are ready, you may feel it merge into your dominant hand, ready to be called upon when next you enact your work. From now on, you can use this scepter of art in place of the prana mudra if you wish. The scepter of art is your true scepter. It goes with you wherever you go and acts as a conduit—a focusing lens for your will. Much of the work you will do with eidolons further on in this book is not confined to a formal ritual circle, and as such, the infinitely portable scepter of art will be an indispensable tool.

Next you will create a physical housing for your scepter of art, known as a scepter of artifice. Before doing so, however, you will first be instructed in the creation of an anointing oil to aid you in that endeavor.

Anointing with Abramelin Oil

Abramelin oil is a traditional anointing oil in ceremonial magic. It is used to consecrate a physical item or space to the service of the great work of magic. You will use it in the creation of a physical vessel for your scepter of art. This oil is called "new-world" Abramelin oil because it adds one ingredient native to South America to the traditional formula, which is otherwise composed of "old-world" ingredients. Please note that if you cannot find these oils, you can complete the ritual with pure olive oil, which is perfectly acceptable even though it will not give the same unique scent that can serve as a sensory aid to entering a ritual state. If you go the route of pure olive oil, simply bottle it in the same manner you would Abramelin oil and exercise your will accordingly.

There are two formulas for this oil: strong and diffused. Strong oil is meant for the consecration of magical tools specifically, and diffused oil is for the working of everyday magic when you wish to incorporate anointing into your ritual design. The ingredient ratios for both are as follows:

- 1 part calamus oil
- 1 part cassia oil
- ½ part cinnamon oil
- 1 part copaiba oil
- 1 part myrrh oil
- *For strong:* 1½ parts olive oil
- *For diffused:* 6 parts olive oil

To craft the oil, mix the ingredients together in a sturdy glass bottle, preferably of clear or blue glass. Upon the bottle, etch, paint, or draw upon a label the following symbol:

Abramelin Oil Symbol

Place the bottle in the middle of a window or outside, at night when the moon and stars are visible. Draw up energy, and feel it run down your arm as you have in your space-setting rituals. The white energy becomes a bright silver as it flows from your fingertips into the bottle and resides there, drinking in the light of the moon and charging an intention for purity. Leave the bottle sitting in view of the moon until dawn. It will then be ready for use.

After you have created your oil, keep it in a cool, dark place, such as a cabinet, closet, or chest, when not being used. Aside from ritual anointing, you may wish to use this oil in a diffuser or on a pumice stone during rituals.

Now that your new-world Abramelin oil is made, you may use it in the ritual to create your scepter of artifice. This ritual connects the scepter of art to an anchor point, the scepter of artifice, that exists in the physical world and channels your scepter of art so that you may concentrate on other details.

The Scepter of Artifice

The scepter of artifice is the physical vessel for your scepter of art, and it is an anchor for it that is mostly used in formal ritual work. While your scepter of art goes with you everywhere, your scepter of artifice is a physical object that you may not wish to cart around from day to day. The recommended dimensions for a scepter of artifice are roughly as long as your arm, from wrist to shoulder, and roughly as thick in diameter as your index and middle fingers side by side. This recommendation is not a hard-and-fast requirement, however. Whatever is most comfortable for you is fine; although, a scepter by nature should generally be longer than a wand and shorter than a staff. When it comes to material, any wood, stone, metal, or combination thereof will suffice. The only ill-advised materials are human-made compounds, such as plastics, because they do not usually conduct energy as readily as materials that have developed in nature. Brittle or easily broken materials, such as glass, wax, and selenite, are also to be shied away from for durability's sake. The scepter of artifice can be as cheap to produce as a painted stick, or as lavish as a rod of solid silver, and it will not affect its potency whatsoever. It is merely a physical anchor for your true scepter.

The first task in creating your scepter of artifice is to procure it. Some magicians prefer to make their own, while some prefer to purchase from an artisan. When purchasing, it is generally a better idea to buy from an independent artist than to select something mass produced simply because you will receive something that has already been treated with reverence by a creator possessing their own will rather than something stamped out by an insentient machine. Once you have obtained your scepter of artifice, anoint it with a few drops of new-world Abramelin oil upon its surface, and let it sit beside an open window from dawn on one day to dawn on the next—one full day and night.

Once you have procured and anointed your scepter of artifice, you will once again set your space with one of the sanctifying circle rituals described earlier in this book, or one of your own design. This time, you will be using your scepter of art in place of the prana mudra. During the casting of the circle, you will keep your scepter of artifice laid out in front of you in the direction you began the ritual facing, ideally upon an altar, or at least with a cloth between it and the ground. When your circle is complete, lift the scepter of artifice with your nondominant hand and hold it straight up in front of you at arm's length. At the same time, raise your dominant arm and envision your scepter of art being held within your dominant hand. Hold it parallel to your scepter of artifice. Envision your scepter of art reaching out to your scepter of artifice and drawing it in, making a connection. Perhaps you will envision it sending out tendrils of electric energy, a field of light, or intricate vines. However you may visualize it, know that your scepter of art is forming a connection with its anchor.

After a few minutes of this visualization, begin to slowly bring your hands together, envisioning the scepter of art glowing brighter as it comes closer to your scepter of artifice. Eventually clasp your dominant hand around the scepter of artifice, and envision the two scepters merging. You should now have both hands around your scepter of artifice. Hold the two scepters together for a few moments, feeling them intermingle and connect. When you feel the connection has been forged, slowly pull your hands apart again, this time holding your scepter of artifice in your dominant hand, and visualize that a hazy imprint of the scepter of art is now superimposed over the scepter of artifice.

Your scepter of artifice is now a ready housing for your scepter of art. Whenever you grasp it in your dominant hand, your scepter of art will flow through it without impediment. From now on in this book, when an exercise instructs you to use your scepter, know that it can be used with or without its physical housing. As a rule, if you have the time and space to call the quarters and create a full circle, your scepter of artifice can be used. Otherwise, it is best to use your scepter of art without its physical conduit.

Having established your scepter, you should take the time to reflect on its creation in your working book. Make note of what it looks like, what sensations you associate with it, and what visualizations took form as you created it. If, at any time, you wish to change your scepter of art, you need simply repeat the first ritual. Similarly if you lose or damage your scepter of artifice (which I hope you do not, but life does have a way of happening to physical objects), you may simply repeat the second ritual to establish a new anchor. It is best to store your scepter of artifice in a place of its own where it will not become damaged, such as upon an altar on a cloth or cushion or in a padded box or chest.

Creating a Cipher

Ciphers have been used by magicians throughout written history to codify their work and keep their secrets from prying eyes. They consist of symbol or number formulas that correlate to letters in the alphabet, words, or phrases. Ciphers can range from the simple to the incredibly complex. In the days when magical study was outlawed by narrow-minded governments, keeping a cipher was a measure of protection that could disguise the magician's notes as a simple ledger. In this era, that is not as much of a concern in most places where you are able to purchase this book. However, when it comes to working with eidolons, there is much you may wish to keep occluded from others, specifically the names of the eidolons. As you will find later, a name that is revealed to you by an eidolon should only be shared if it has given consent for you to do so. Think of it like sharing a friend's phone number. It is not something you would want to do with just any stranger. I have provided two simple ciphers: a cipher that correlates letters of the alphabet to alchemical symbols, and one that uses the positions of letters on a grid to generate symbols for those letters. These are only examples; it is highly recommended that you develop your own as these examples will be known to all who have read this book.

A	B	C	D	E
F	G	H	I	J
K	L	M	N	O
P	Q	R	S	T
U	V	W	X	Y
Z				

"Cipher"

Alchemical Cipher

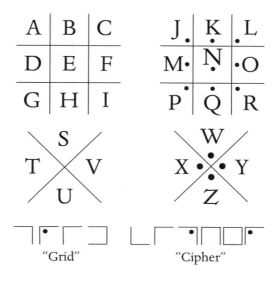

Grid Cipher

Using these ciphers, or preferably similar ones of your own design, will afford you some privacy in your work should your tome fall under prying eyes. Hopefully, this will prove an unnecessary precaution for you.

The Circle of Concentric Ascension

You now possess a fully realized scepter. Congratulations. You have undergone the regular exercises necessary to ground and expand your awareness and your being. You have filled your tome with observations on the various meditations and concepts introduced here. Perhaps you have sketched your scepter of art in your tome, or handcrafted your scepter of artifice. Regardless of the exact specifics, if you have made it this far and have taken to heart the techniques and instructions of this book, you are ready to take your next step and refer to yourself as an adept, one who has come into the practice of a working magician in this system. After the following dedication ritual, you will be on the path to mastery. It is one that takes lifetimes to culminate but provides the seeker with much enrichment along the way.

The Circle of Concentric Ascension describes both a ritual and the specific ritual circle in which it takes place. If you have the space, the circle can be drawn upon the floor. If not, having it on a large piece of paper set before you will also suffice.

For this ritual, you will need the following circle. You will notice it contains the word *Lord*, which evokes a personified deity. This is not necessary, and it can be interchanged with *spirit, destiny, universe, potential,* or any word that more accurately meshes with your operating paradigm.

Circle of Concentric Ascension

You will begin by holding your scepter of artifice in your dominant hand and calling the quarters with the exercise of your choice. After this you will stand (if your circle is on the floor) or focus (if your circle is on paper or in your tome) on the eye at the center of the circle. Raise your scepter before you and say as follows:

"I stand at the hub of the wheel, the eye of the maelstrom, the fulcrum of the scale."

At this point, you will anoint your forehead with a small drop of new-world Abramelin oil or pure olive oil using your dominant thumb or index finger, whichever is easier while holding your scepter.

Turn your attention to the first square of the octagram and feel the four elements of the cardinal directions dancing upon their corresponding points. Raise your scepter before you and say as follows:

"At the cardinal corners I invoke the four material gates, that their energies may flow freely through me and find harmony within me."

The four material gates represent the four classical elements of fire, water, earth, and air and, in turn, the world of matter.

Next turn your attention to the second square of the octagram and to the four elements between directions on their corresponding points. Raise your scepter before you and say as follows:

"At the in-between places I invoke the four immaterial gates, that their energies may flow freely through me and find harmony within me."

The four immaterial gates represent the transubstantive elements of light, darkness, life, and death and, in turn, the immaterial world.

Finally, turn your attention to the triangle that surrounds the eye in the middle of the circle. Raise your scepter above your head in your dominant hand and hold your nondominant arm down at your side, hand open and palm facing forward with fingertips pointed at the ground. Say as follows:

"I invoke the ninth gate, the unity gate from which all things flow, the one that is many, the source of all things. Flow through me that I may ascend to the apex of the great work. Fashion me into an instrument of the highest good. Protect me that I may abide with the eidolons. Judge me should I willingly stray from the path of harmony. Heal me should I be led into discord."

The ninth gate represents the quintessence of spirit and is representative of standing in perfect harmony with the elements of the previous eight gates.

Strike the bottom of your scepter upon the ground (not too hard), and read aloud the words on the perimeter of the circle:

"Lord lift us up to do thy work."

As mentioned in the beginning of this ritual, *Lord* can be replaced with *spirit, universe, destiny, potential, positivity,* or any other word of significance to you at your preference. The *us* in this invocation refers to you and all magicians who have come before and will come after.

At this point you may wish to stand and abide in the emotions and sensations this ritual evokes within you and allow any available messages or visualizations to flow through your consciousness. At the very least, take a few deep breaths before proceeding to close your circle in the way you have become accustomed to, ending with the closing phrase "So it is," or any similar phrase of your choosing, and slowly allowing the ritual visualization to fade.

You will want to make detailed notes of this experience in your tome. It is indicative of your crossing a boundary and stepping over a threshold to dedicate yourself to the art of magic. It will likely mark a turning point for you, and you will find your work taking on a new depth. As such, it is good to mark that point. If, at any point, you feel you are wavering, or you simply wish to restate your dedication to the art, this ritual can be repeated.

Having passed through the Circle of Concentric Ascension, you now stand in the antechamber of the eidolons. From here you are prepared to interface with these intelligences at the appropriate level of receptivity.

Chapter 5
SEAL, SIGIL,
AND CALL

If you have been following along closely and doing the work in each chapter thus far, you have passed through the nine gates of the Circle of Concentric Ascension. Congratulations, adept. Now you have come to the core of this work. All that you have previously done has prepared you for what is to come.

In the following pages, you will develop what is referred to in this system as an ark. It is a list of nonphysical entities, called eidolons, that will fill much of your tome, each entity having a name, a seal, and a sigil through which you may contact them. You will be introduced to the conceptual framework of contacting and summoning eidolons, the preparatory essentials, and information on eidolons amenable to being contacted. These eidolons, the core group referred to as the inner host of the ark, are present in the arks of all magicians of this system. Beyond them, it is my hope that you will, as I have, contact a whole cavalcade of interesting and beneficent eidolons through your own illuminations.

On Contacting Eidolons

In this system, we define an eidolon as any nonphysical, self-aware entity that has never been incarnated as a biological creature on earth. Or alternatively, entities that inhabit the subconscious mind. This classification includes many entities of various vicissitudes. However, the main three classifications with which we are concerned are otherworld spirits, primals, and celestials. Eidolons can straddle or overlap these classifications, and you may find the way that you classify the ones that you work with will change as your understanding of them changes.

Otherworld spirits are the eidolons who occupy a similar band of existence to the one in which we live. This is to say, they are roughly equivalent in quality and frequency (but not magnitude) of energy to our own. Otherworld spirits include elementals, fey, and a host of many gods and goddesses, among many other wondrous and mysterious manifestations of consciousness. These eidolons are perhaps the most readily available to contact. These entities could also be viewed as parts of the psyche close to the conscious mind, embodying concepts that are easily quantified and explained with human language.

Primals are the eidolons who occupy a lower vibrational band of existence than the one in which we live. We do not use *lower* as a hierarchical designation here but as a tonal value. These are chthonic entities representative of the deeper unconscious and the mysterious pre-existential chaos. These eidolons can be difficult to communicate with without practice, and they usually require unambiguous phrasing when addressing. These entities can also be viewed as parts of the psyche deep in the subconscious mind.

Celestials are the eidolons who occupy a higher vibrational band of existence than we do. The archangels fall squarely into this category. They exist in a plane of manifestation that vibrates in a bright, clear manner. These eidolons are idealized entities, having already achieved their higher selves. Ascended magicians and other ascended spiritual seekers occupy this category, as do many deities; they are highly intuitive and will often understand the true meaning behind your words even when you may not. These entities can also be associated with aspirational psychological qualities and positive spiritual manifestations, such as compassion, justice, wisdom, and love.

To aid in classification, the closer to human interaction you can have with an eidolon, the more likely it can be classified as an otherworld spirit. The more that communication becomes conveyed through emotion, sensation, and cryptic imagery, the more likely the eidolon can be classified as a primal. Finally, the more communication becomes like the direct transfer of clear ideas into your consciousness in the form of inspiration, the more likely the eidolon can be classified as a celestial.

Keep in mind that these categories are not sacred or inviolate. They are merely working categories to aid the magician in classifying the eidolons of their ark. You may, and likely will, develop subcategories as you progress. Perhaps you will choose new classifications altogether or eschew classification in its entirety. Your practice should be tailored to suit your own needs.

The name an eidolon gives is much like a phone number or email address. It is a mode of instant communication. Unlike in human society, an eidolon's name is often the last thing you will discover about it unless you have been introduced to it by another magician. The first concrete notion you will usually receive from an eidolon is their seal. If an eidolon's name is a phone number, their seal is their mailing address. You will use their seal as a meditation focus to gradually learn more about them. You will also develop a call, or a short phrase that you will use to send your will toward them along with their name. Using a telecommunications metaphor again, if an eidolon's name is their phone number, then a call is the phone through which you establish contact. Finally, as your association with an eidolon becomes more familiar, you will assign a small and easily drawn symbol to them, a sigil, which will act as a physical token you may use as a focus for communication. Using seals, sigils, and calls, you can enact all of your necessary communications with the eidolons you meet.

It is important to take a moment to speak about privacy before we continue. It is a grave breach of the working relationship a magician shares with the eidolons they know to distribute their contact information without their consent. As with any friend, you wouldn't give someone's contact information to strangers without their approval. The eidolons gathered in this book were specifically selected as being open to contact from magicians, and even then, none of the names they have given me are shared. It is up to you, the reader, to reach out using their seals and sigils and see if they are willing to work with you.

You may first perceive an eidolon as a notion, a feeling, or a vision. Meditating on that first touch point will eventually reveal to you an eidolon's seal, which is a perfect circle containing symbols or patterns within that are representative of that eidolon. You will scribe that seal in your tome and take it into your circle, touch the seal with your scepter, and further reflect on it. It may take multiple attempts, but eventually, in the eidolon's own time, it will reveal itself to you. You will speak, and you may part before hearing its name, but do not be discouraged. Eidolons, like people, come in all kinds of personalities and points of view. You must work with them to understand them and earn their trust. Having an ark full of eidolons whom you barely know is not as desirable as having a handful of eidolons with whom you share a close connection. Of course, having an ark of many eidolons with whom you share a close bond is an aspirational goal.

Eventually, you will learn the name of the eidolon you are working with, and you will scribe it in your tome. When you make a page for an eidolon, it is best to leave a space at the top of the page for its name. However, remember, you should write its name in cipher. An eidolon's name should only be shared if it has given its consent to be introduced to other magicians. This sharing is done through copying the pages of your tome onto sheets of paper or cards to be gifted to other magicians or traded among any practitioner's circle you may belong to.

When you have been engaged in this work for a bit and have contacted your first several eidolons, you may notice that you receive answers more quickly, or even receive an eidolon's name outright or before its seal. Take this as a sign that you are growing as a practitioner, and thank the eidolon for its vote of confidence.

Calling Eidolons

Through working with an eidolon, you will assign them a sigil, which is a simple call sign that associates with them in your mind. This is used as a shortcut for calling that eidolon along with their name. A sigil can be a small symbol written on a piece of paper or on an actual object, such as a small bell, bit of bone, or crystal. For ease of use, it is recommended that you draw an eidolon's sigil on a slip of paper when calling them, rather than carry around several bulkier trinkets as representations. However, the choice is your own.

Once you have an eidolon's name, you will be able to call upon them even outside of formal ritual, and indeed, this is most of the work you will do once your practice matures. Meditating on seals, discovering eidolons' names, and assigning them sigils can be considered the process of agreeing to work together. Past that, the actual work begins. You will find each eidolon has their own specialties in terms of tasks and goals they can help you accomplish, knowledge they can impart, and lengths to which they are willing to go to assist you. The last item on that list largely depends on the relationship you have forged with each eidolon.

To call an eidolon, you should envision their seal in your mind's eye, hold their sigil, and call their name along with whatever call phrase you have discovered. Eidolon calls can be organized as you wish, but the general formula I adhere to is this:

> *"{Name and/or epithet(s) of the eidolon}, I stand in a circle of my own design and call you by {phrase, concept, or thematic conceit of importance to the eidolon}. Will you {entreat/collaborate/commune/abide} with me?"*

You do want to be in a circle when doing this to prevent uninvited entities from dropping in on your energized space. However, you need not cast a full formal circle. Instead, you can envision an instantaneous circle around you, a circle of your own design. You will bring this circle to the surface of your mind, visualizing it on the floor or in the air around you, turning away any influence from your work.

Here we take the word *design* to mean will. This phrase, used in all eidolon invocations, means that you stand in a circle composed of your own will. You may visualize this in any way you would like. If you are unsure of what visualization to employ, a triangle within a circle within a square is a strong visual option. Perhaps envision it springing into life in purple fire or glowing like a sun. What is important is that you draw deep on the root connection you have established through your centering

exercises and allow the unfettered energy of existence that you have practiced abiding within to flow around you and manifest in your circle.

"I stand in a circle of my own design ..."

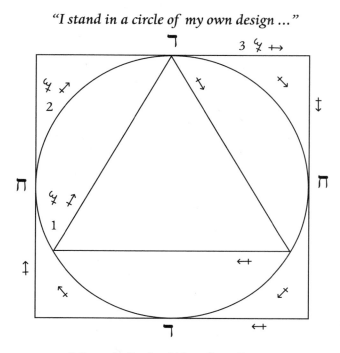

A Sample Circle of Your Own Design

The Inner Host of the Ark

The host of the ark refers to all the eidolons that reside within a magician's
ark, which is our word for the section of our tomes dedicated to catalog-
ing eidolons. This section need not be contiguous, nor even confined to
one tome. It is simply to be understood that this is what you are referring
to when you reference your ark; it is the collection of all eidolons known
to you. The inner host refers to the collection of eighteen eidolons refer-
enced in this book, which all practitioners may include in their personal
arks. It is advised you attempt contact with at least half of the eidolons
comprising the inner host—and successfully work with at least three—
before moving on to searching for new eidolons to contact.

To begin working with the inner host, you may select an eidolon's seal and attempt to make contact in what should be considered the standard way briefly described earlier, which is as follows. You will begin by meditating on its seal and reaching out with your will. During this meditation you will hold the eidolon's sigil and utter its call. The seals, sigils, and calls for the eighteen eidolons of the inner host are all provided in the following pages. The call may include the eidolon's name, an epithet, or simply a placeholder that describes how you met it or a quality you associate with it. Keep in mind that the name one magician is given may not be the same another is given, and this is both valid and expected. Using a name in a call is as much a way for an eidolon to identify you as it is for you to identify them, as they remember what names they give to whom. It is also understood that no names of the inner host of the ark should be given to other magicians under any circumstances, as contacting these first eighteen eidolons is a rite of passage and should not be denied or circumvented with shortcuts. In addition, this is a grave breach of protocol and can result in an eidolon becoming difficult to work with or unresponsive in the future. Many of the eidolons of the inner host make excellent guides to your practice once a relationship of mutual consideration is developed.

Consider each eidolon entry in the inner host of the ark to be a blueprint for the entries of all the eidolons you will contact in the future. Each entry will include a space for the eidolons name (in this book the name is replaced by the number of the eidolon entry), or the name itself where already revealed, a seal, a description that denotes how the eidolon appeared to you and what its specialties are, and a description denoting how its sigil appears when drawn on paper. Keep in mind that the inner host entries are all complete, but as you contact new eidolons you will be filling in your tome bit by bit as you discover more about them.

In the following section, we will refer to some eidolons with gendered pronouns. This only reflects the gender expression they have most often chosen to use in dealings with me. Eidolons are not bound by physical matter and can choose to express their identities in any conceivable way. They are beings of pure energy consciousness and are not bound by the preconceptions or categorizations of the material world or its inhabitants.

Along this same avenue, it is important to dispense of the myth of a "true" form. Consciousness, whether incarnated in we humans or free and flowing, as with the eidolons, is formless, nameless, and timeless. All layers of form and nomenclature are worn as vestments by consciousness and are as easily discarded. While forms are listed for the following eidolon descriptions, it is due to them having appeared this way on numerous occasions to me. These forms often vary slightly, even in one magician's practice from day to day, and they can be changed by an eidolon at whim to convey changes in mood, purpose, or simply preference. The reason they are included at all is to give the beginner a reference point from which to visualize if desired.

It is also important to clarify that many of the eidolons to follow are referred to as presiding or having dominion over certain concepts or themes. This is not to say they rule or own these things on an existential level but rather to denote that these are the concepts with which they are associated in this ark. Eidolons will interact with different magicians in different ways, and the manner of assistance and abilities they offer will vary from magician to magician.

It is recommended that you read through all eighteen eidolon entries and find the one that resonates most strongly with you before deciding which one to attempt contact with first. Further information on contacting eidolons can be found in the section titled Utilizing Eidolon Entries, which comes directly after the eighteenth eidolon entry.

The First Eidolon

The first eidolon is an otherworld spirit. They style themselves a divinity of life, song, merriment, and joy. Their sigil is the image of a lyre, drawn simply, and they can be called while holding it by the song in one's heart. For example:

"{Name}, laughing lord of melody, I stand in a circle of my own design and call you by the song in my heart. Will you entreat with me?"

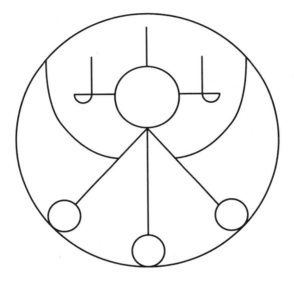

Seal of the First Eidolon

The first eidolon most often appears as a joyful, elfin figure clad in bright colors and bearing an instrument, usually stringed. While they have most often appeared to me as a young male, they have made it clear that they tend to match their appearance to the gender expression of the magician. This is to facilitate an atmosphere of peer-ship. They enjoy interacting in a convivial, casual, and supportive manner. The first eidolon seeks to inspire the magician to create, explore, and feel joy. Their chief lesson is to see life incarnated in the material world as a blessing and a chance to explore myriad sensations and appreciate innumerable beauties.

The first eidolon can be considered an impresario of sorts. They delight in aiding in any endeavor of the arts or act of merriment and exude a sense of joie de vivre. Being perhaps the most effusively and demonstratively friendly of the eidolons on this list, they are oftentimes eager to introduce you to other eidolons whose presence they feel you will benefit from. These eidolons are likely to be otherworld spirits of a similar bent to themselves. They often describe these friends as being members of what we would call a pantheon, though not one of any earthly faith or historical reckoning and not one that seeks worship or fealty.

The first eidolon makes an excellent guide, the role of which is explained in chapter 6, as they are always happy to speak with potential friends and introduce them to others.

Listening for the First Eidolon

As with all eidolons, your first foray into contacting this eidolon should center around meditating on their seal while in a ritual circle. It is highly likely that this initial meditation will have no tangible result. Do not be discouraged. Once you have been working with eidolons for some time, these initial contacts will be more immediately fruitful. For now, however, they serve as introductions. Allow the eidolon you are attempting to contact to be exposed to your energy and evaluate how well you may work together. For the first eidolon, attempting initial contact in a natural area, particularly near wildflowers, can be beneficial. It may also serve to incorporate a beloved scented oil or incense, piece of music, or even a ritual meal into your attempt. As always, and for all eidolon entries to follow, these are enhancements rather than necessities.

The skill you will need to cultivate to establish reliable contact is the art of listening deeply to existence. Each eidolon has its own unique ways that it prefers to communicate, and much information will be sent to you through subtle whispers of intuition and portent before you ever have what others might classify as a conversation. Here, and in all eidolon entries to follow, you will be given guidance on how the eidolons of the inner host of the ark typically communicate. This is not to say they have no other methods, and their nuances can vary between magicians, but in my experience, each eidolon tends to favor certain modes of contact.

The first eidolon is a highly sensory being and will attempt to make their presence known through calling up memories of floral scents such as honeysuckle, gardenia, or lilac. They will often communicate through song or spoken rhyme. This communication manifests in many ways, but it is important to understand that it is something you feel. Hearing a song being played is not always a communication but hearing a song that strikes a chord in you, that feels heavy with presence, very well may be. Discerning the unique feeling of an eidolon reaching out is one of those skills that can only improve through exposure over time.

That said, as magicians we understand that we must shape our realities. While we cannot ethically or safely force an eidolon to manifest, we can certainly stack the odds in our favor by making sure we put ourselves in situations that give an eidolon ample opportunity to make themselves known to us. As such, when awaiting acknowledgment from the first eidolon, it is particularly useful to engage in activities such as the writing or reading of poetry, listening to music, singing, playing an instrument, arranging flowers, savoring a favorite food or drink, walking through a botanical garden, or attending a lively festival or concert.

The Second Eidolon

The second eidolon is another otherworld spirit, though quite a bit more private than the first you have been introduced to. He refers to himself as a divinity of death, transitions, and liminality. He is a patron of spiritual seekers and those who pursue obscure or hidden knowledge. He can be called by the shadow on the threshold or the lantern at the crossroad. His sigils are the lantern and the hand sickle. Either of these may be drawn simply upon paper and held in the hand when calling him.

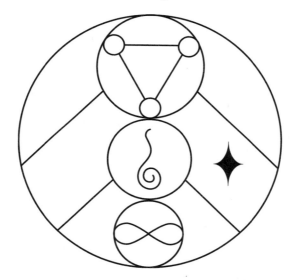

Seal of the Second Eidolon

The second eidolon, much as the first and unlike many to follow, often appears as an elfin figure of humanoid proportions. His body is often wrapped in black fabric, as if mummified, and adorned with flowing funerary robes of similar black silken cloth. He holds in his right hand a unique harvesting implement that he describes as something used to pull fruit from branches in another world or dimension. It is a small sharpened hook on a long pole. This object appears to be something he regards as a badge of office and, whatever form he may take, it is usually incorporated. When he visits, he is often accompanied by many floating lanterns of various cool hues of blue, purple, and teal. These lanterns are meant to be guideposts for the spirits of the recently departed and are symbolic of his role as a psychopomp.

The second eidolon is calm in temperament and soft spoken; he speaks concisely. He is a keen observer and will often understand details and nuances in the magician's speech and mannerism that the magician may not even be personally aware of.

While all eidolons can assist and enrich you in myriad ways, the second eidolon is especially adept at and enthusiastic about assisting in manners of introspection. He is at home in silence and can help foster inner calm, silencing the voices of anxiety, self-doubt, and fear. He is also eager to engage in any research, as the uncovering of knowledge is something he values highly. To this end, he presides over a specific advanced divination method that may be covered in future works. He is a boon companion to any divination at all.

Another key task the second eidolon is happy to set himself to is to help process grief over loss and alleviate fear of death. He very much wishes to aid physical beings in coming to a true understanding that consciousness is eternal and death is a transitory phase. The first and second eidolons together impart the lesson that one should drink deeply from the cup of life, knowing that one day death will come, and that in knowing this, one should assure they do good that will outlast their time on this physical world.

Listening for the Second Eidolon

Unlike the first eidolon before him, establishing initial contact with the second eidolon is best done in calm, silent places. The dim light of candles or lanterns, especially colorful paper lanterns, is conducive to this work, as is the presence of slowly burning resins such as myrrh or copal. The second eidolon rarely communicates in a sensory nature. Instead, he often communicates in emotional waves of calm or suddenly recalled memories of loved ones who have passed.

The second eidolon enjoys establishing contact in sacred places, especially ones of significant age, and will often communicate when near shrines. He can also be roused to interest while engaged in divination work. The second eidolon will rarely answer your request for initial contact in loud, harshly lit, or crowded places. Other areas where his presence can be felt easily are liminal spaces, such as railways stations, airports, subway cars, and rest stops on highways, all during off-hours when they are most sparsely peopled.

The Third Eidolon

The third eidolon is the first primal of the host, and it remains one of the most difficult of the eighteen contained in this book to deal with in a manner that resembles everyday human interaction. This eidolon's sigil is the scarab, or a stinging insect, drawn in black. He is the bringer and mitigator of swarms and pestilences, ruler over chitinous things, and lord of wasps, locusts, and scorpions. He is often called the lord of the swarm and can be called by the wing of the locust, the droning of the swarm, or the one that is many.

Seal of the Third Eidolon

The third eidolon often appears as a pale and emaciated human male, wearing a beaten and tattered kilt-like garment of mildewed leather around his waist. Like many of the winged figures of the host, he usually wears nothing on his torso. He possesses an insectoid left arm and great wings that appear as birds' wings. Instead of feathers, they are pinioned by large dragonfly wings. His lower face is often covered by a gas mask, cloth, or menpō.

Despite his sinister appearance, the third eidolon is not a hostile entity. No such entities have been listed in this book intended for new adepts.

However, unlike the first and second eidolons, he is not particularly beneficent either. Rather, he is concerned very much with crawling, chittering, and stinging things. He is not an avid conversationalist and tends to respond with gestures and waves of emotion more than ideas that can be formed into words.

All of this said, the third eidolon does possess a great deal of knowledge, as he has observed much of this world's natural history through the faceted eyes of his charges. He knows much of the life cycles and habits of insects and arachnids. If coaxed into speech by interest in this subject, he will regale you with musings on all manner of crawling things, and if spoken to clearly, he may be willing to help you drive away wasps or other insects so that they may not run afoul of humans and meet their end. He also has access to an infinite number of literal flies on the walls, and as such, he can collect a vast amount of observational knowledge if he turns his will to this end.

As with all primals, the third eidolon must be spoken to with little ambiguity. He will take what you say literally, as he is a creature who occupies a more rigid, more slowly vibrating band of existence. Several primals described here are unable to understand nuanced communication to the level that otherworld spirits or celestials can. They often have less common ground with humans to infer from and require unambiguous statements rather than metaphor. Contacting the third eidolon is a serviceable foray into speaking with primals since, if mistakes are made, he is far more likely to turn away disinterested than to take any offense.

Listening for the Third Eidolon

Making first contact with the third eidolon may be somewhat difficult for squeamish people, as he will almost invariably do so through the flight patterns of bees, wasps, or hornets when available in the magician's area. If such creatures are unavailable, he will communicate through the movement of other insects, especially ants. This is not to say every sighting of a chitinous creature will be a subtle communication from the third eidolon, but you may feel his presence through such things at times. He will pay close attention to how you treat such creatures, especially bees, when they cross your path, though he understands the need for humans to shun more parasitic insects, such as mosquitoes and ticks.

Creating ideal conditions for the third eidolon to answer your invitation for first contact may be the most difficult of any of the inner host of the ark. Keep in mind ideal conditions are an encouragement, not a necessity. I would posit that the ideal place to listen for the third eidolon would be an apiary, but I do not advise that anyone aside from a trained beekeeper wander around apiaries. Indeed, a beekeeper would have the perfect profession for developing a strong bond with the third eidolon. Alternatively, one may seek out places to observe insects going about their daily lives. This can be something as commonplace as observing a few bumblebees in a yard. Keeping an ant farm or an insect pet, such as a stag beetle, could also serve to connect you more closely to the third eidolon and invite many opportunities to receive his messages.

The Fourth Eidolon

The fourth eidolon is a primal whose sigil is the black seed or onyx disk. He is a keeper of many mysteries lost to time, the secrets of long-dead civilizations, and truths locked in the unconscious mind. He holds power over darkness and, to a degree, entropy. Once first contact is made, he is most easily spoken to in utter darkness. He is a master of chthonic magic and the manifestation of symbolic things into physical reality.

Seal of the Fourth Eidolon

The fourth eidolon appears as a tall, four-armed man with jet-black skin. His posture is regal, and he is dressed as an Akkadian priest in white and gold. Above his head floats a golden crown in the shape of a ziggurat, and on either side of his head, at his temples, hovers a bright green crystalline obelisk about a hand's length high. He is often adorned in elaborate golden jewelry.

Unlike the third eidolon before him, the fourth eidolon is well versed in human conversation. He delights in stories and myths and is eager to hear of your work and offer anecdotes about ancient mages. However, unlike the second eidolon, he is motivated more by the collection of knowledge than its dissemination.

The fourth eidolon is an especially expert aid in the manifestation of your will in distant places, and he can be sent forth to enact your aims in remote locales. He is also a boon companion in meditations where the goal is pulling forth manifested signs or wisdoms from the depths of the unconscious mind. As such, he is an excellent partner in the listening meditation you will be introduced to in chapter 8.

The fourth eidolon is a fiercely curious entity and one who forms bonds readily with dedicated magicians. He is likely to be dismissive of those he deems as merely dabbling and holds a particular regard for those who have been practicing the arts arcane for multiple lifetimes, with whom he feels a kinship. This temperament leads him to seek carte blanche to enter the magician's space at will and observe their magical workings. As such, he is often happy to fill the role of a guide.

The fourth eidolon can be called by the darkness beyond the stars.

Listening for the Fourth Eidolon

Listening for the fourth eidolon is best done, perhaps obviously, in total darkness. He tends to make his presence known through surges of magical inspiration and feelings of profound curiosity about the nature of existence. He is also likely to make his presence known in the ambient sounds of a library or museum or in the night noises of a busy university fallen quiet after hours. He may draw your attention to a line in a book left open in a bookstore or a phrase left on a university whiteboard.

The fourth eidolon is one of the easier eidolons of the inner host to listen for. He is drawn to magical work, and for a magician, opportunities to hear his answer to your first request for contact should abound. He can also be heard in shops that cater to the metaphysical, occult, and magical; perhaps in something as mundane as a door's chime or as subtle as the scent of a freshly printed book. You may detect the nascent darkness just beyond the scrim of the world of forms and feel a looming height reading over your shoulder.

The Fifth Eidolon

The next of this host of eighteen eidolons, the fifth eidolon, straddles a classificational line. He could be categorized as either an otherworld spirit or a primal. He possesses traits of a primal insofar as he is unambiguous in his dealings and concerned very keenly with a specific focus, the knitting of wounds and the systems of the physical body, to the point of single-mindedness. However, it is also clear that he is capable of varied and nuanced interactions when he chooses to step away from his persistent fascination with the healing of ailments of physical forms. As such, he is classified as an otherworld spirit, albeit one with a tendency to hyper fix-ate to the point of ignoring conversations that do not involve his singular passion.

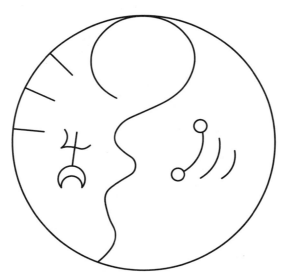

Seal of the Fifth Eidolon

The fifth eidolon's sigil is the gnarled staff or cane. He is a benevolent physician and soother of ailments. He is a sagacious counselor on physiol-ogy, biology, and pharmacology, and he is delighted to assist in the study of such things. He is a purifier and warder against poisonous spirits, pro-jected ill will, and other forms of toxicity. He can be called by the healing bough or the waters of life.

The fifth eidolon often appears as an old, thin man with the head of a black vulture. He usually wears a white shendyt and bears a crooked cane. Although he is incapable of smiling in this form, he projects the air of a kindly elder and his knowing smile can be felt beyond visual need for it. A rare departure from his preoccupation with various healing arts, the fifth eidolon is also fond of giving general life advice in the way an elder might to the children of their community. He may see this in and of itself as a form of healing—healing traumas, healing behavioral patterns learned in the material world, and helping foster a sense of acceptance.

Listening for the Fifth Eidolon

When sending your first invitation through meditating on the fifth eidolon's seal, it is beneficial to do so while having fresh medicinal herbs around you and while in a clean and orderly room. Burning white candles and dried herbs can also set the appropriate ambience for the fifth eidolon, who wishes for an environment of healing. After having done so, there are many ways that the fifth eidolon may make himself known initially before eventually conversing with you.

The fifth eidolon is likely to communicate his answer to your first invitation in pharmacies, hospitals, or even veterinary offices. Similarly, he will be comfortable in the demesnes of many places where traditional healing is practiced. He will cast his presence upon you in the sounds of medical devices, the scents of aromatherapy, and the feeling of relief when a tense muscle relaxes. He will also communicate in the movements and calls of birds, especially corvids and vultures.

The Sixth Eidolon

The sixth eidolon is an otherworld spirit who knows of hidden treasures and bestows luck in obtaining them. They love, above all, things of aesthetic beauty. They are particularly effusive about sculpture, jewelry, and precious metalwork.

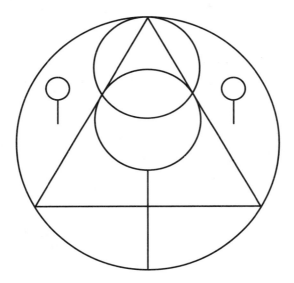

Seal of the Sixth Eidolon

The sixth eidolon encourages those who would produce precious things, and as such, they are a natural patron of jewelers, sculptors, and painters. They also are greatly concerned with the preservation of ancient works of art and are a friend to conservators, restorers, and archivists. The sixth eidolon is a great lover of gems and minerals and can aid in locating, appraising, and working with them.

This otherworld spirit most often appears as an androgynous youth with hair as woven gold, beautiful rainbow wings in place of arms, and the lower body of an emerald serpent from the waist down. Often, this eidolon appears with a large golden harp that they play seemingly by thought alone. They are adept at the technique of tonal resonance, which is described in chapter 8.

The sigil of the sixth eidolon is a keyhole, and they can be called by the glimmer through the keyhole or the chisel of the sculptor.

The sixth eidolon can be wrathful to those who seek to use their aid to avaricious end. They disdain those who hoard objects of beauty, not sharing that beauty so it may be admired by many. In addition, they cannot abide destruction as a means of attaining beautiful things. As such, they are innately opposed to destructive or exploitative mining and deeply frown upon stealing works of art from their creators.

Listening for the Sixth Eidolon

Establishing your first contact request with the sixth eidolon is best done when surrounded by things of crafted beauty, such as sculptures or paintings, or by precious and semiprecious stones. An art museum or crystal cave would be ideal, but unfortunately, they are not private enough for a first contact ritual. String music, especially from a harp, can also be helpful.

Listening for the sixth eidolon is similarly best done when surrounded by beauty, and this requires much less privacy than the ritual itself. Walk the halls of an art museum or gallery, take in the glinting facets of a gem exhibit, or wander a sculpture garden to be moved by the presence of the sixth eidolon. The sixth eidolon will often establish a first sign of contact in breathtaking moments in which you are truly touched by something beautiful, as well as in sudden urges to create artistically. They are also prone to offer inspirations to seek lost items or participate in scavenger hunts, geocaching, or other activities in which the aim is to find something hidden.

The Seventh Eidolon

The seventh eidolon is an otherworld spirit who is a master of military strategy and knower of the secrets of the desert. He is even tempered and imperious, and he aids in the tasks of just command, logistics, and organization. He is related to the sixth eidolon but not in a way that can be translated to any earthly relationship.

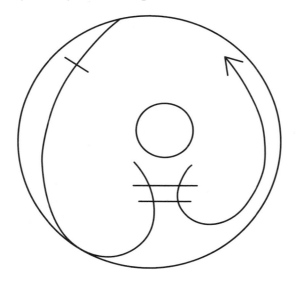

Seal of the Seventh Eidolon

The seventh eidolon aids in matters of self-respect and bearing; his mantra is "every chair a throne." He seeks to help the magician realize their inherent self-worth as an infinite being and, in turn, understand the equal worth of all other sentient life. He is a commander who leads by example, and his regal foundation is a strength of spirit above all.

The seventh eidolon can be called upon to aid the magician in assuming a commanding presence or making their voice heard in a crowd. He can also help in matters of posture, inspiration, and mental fortitude. He is a protective spirit who is vigilant against the forces he finds most aberrant: cowardice, cruelty, exploitation, and other types of pusillanimous behavior, especially on the part of those in positions of authority.

The seventh eidolon appears as a six-armed muscular man with a curved sword in each hand. His head is that of a lion wearing a golden crown, and from his waist downward, his form is that of a ruby serpent. He can be called by the winds of the desert or the medal of office, and his sigil is a crown above a horizontal scimitar.

The seventh eidolon is an imposing presence, and he seeks to help one walk with purpose and live with resolve. He is often silent, simply sticking close to the magician and radiating a powerful force of presence that bids one to stand straight, operate forthrightly, and defend those who fall prey to the cruel and selfish.

Listening for the Seventh Eidolon

When first meditating on the seventh eidolon's seal, it is beneficial to do so while standing straight with shoulders back and head held high. Keeping a sword (if you can handle one safely) or a piece of art depicting a sword (or swords) in your circle may also add to the experience, as would performing the ritual in a desert (if such can be done comfortably). It is also a boon to wear garments or adornments that make you feel confident.

The seventh eidolon is more likely to communicate at certain moments than certain places. Although, he is fond of deserts as well as battlefields. More likely, however, he will make his presence known when you are trying things outside of your comfort zone; engaging in actions that rely on self-discipline, such as exercise or study; or defending those who are being harmed by people in positions of power, especially children and others who find it difficult to defend themselves. He will make his presence known by a dispelling of fear, a welling of confidence, and a desire to defend, his many swords parrying the depredations of those who would assail you.

The Eighth Eidolon

The eighth eidolon is a celestial whose sigil is the telescope or sextant. It knows the movements of heavenly bodies, bestows protections, and delivers auguries of potency and accuracy. It is a patron of astronomers, astrologers, and navigators.

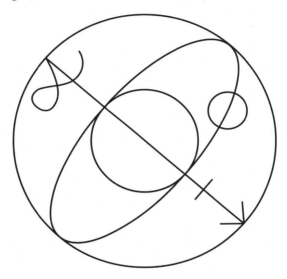

Seal of the Eighth Eidolon

The eighth eidolon is a skilled navigator and pathfinder, able to help you find your metaphorical way when you feel lost or adrift. It is friendly with new magicians who show eagerness to learn and apply their knowledge for the collective universal good. It is exceedingly beneficent, eager to help in spiritual betterment, and very patient.

The eighth eidolon, like most celestials described in this book, is able to help one glimpse the overall geometry of existence and the ineffable patterns of causality and concordance that underpin what we think of as reality. It can lead your soul to walk on paths that you will scarcely be able to articulate upon your return to a physical focal point. Working with celestials is extremely enriching. When working with such beings, prepare yourself to check your assumptions about the nature of reality at the door, so to speak.

The eighth eidolon appears as either a collection of radiant spheres in a complex helical orbit around one another or as a humanoid figure composed of silver light with a tapestry of the night sky draped over its shoulders and a golden sextant in its right hand.

The eighth eidolon can be called by the galactic spiral, the myriad constellations, or the guiding star.

Listening for the Eighth Eidolon

When first meditating upon the seal of the eighth eidolon, it is beneficial to be outside under the starry skies at night in a calm, safe place. I find that camping far from the lights of city and town can be extremely enriching in this regard. If you can see the Milky Way, you are in an ideal spot. Not much else is needed to add to the experience, although the presence of a telescope could be a nice bonus.

The eighth eidolon may be inclined to answer your first contact request while stargazing or studying the movement or symbolism of celestial bodies. However, all celestials share some particular traits when it comes to answering your initial meditation in the days and weeks after the request is made. All celestials, in my experience, will be inclined to answer when you are acting in line with your highest potential for kindness, altruism, and self-betterment.

Celestial eidolons can often be generalized as beings of light; although this is not always the case, it is so often enough to be a useful catchall. The eighth eidolon is no different, and its presence can be described like the feeling of starlight or moonlight cast upon your consciousness. It will lead you to feel a peaceful understanding, a sense that existence is moving, and that that movement is sublime.

The Ninth Eidolon

The ninth eidolon is an otherworld spirit of great and specific power. He is a high pyromancer whose sole delight is flame in all its physical and metaphorical forms. His is the word that ignites and extinguishes candle and conflagration alike, and his is the flame that anoints, purifies, and impassions.

Seal of the Ninth Eidolon

The ninth eidolon has few ways in which to interface with the magician aside from his talent as a conversationalist who waxes philosophical on myriad subjects, dwelling most often on the metaphorical nature of fire. However, he is a boon companion when attempting to divine through fire gazing or when making candles or incense. He is also a protector of firefighters, as his dominion over flame includes its extinguishing.

The ninth eidolon understands the use of fire as a tool for agriculture, a driver of engines, the mother of cooking, and the purifier of elements. He also understands the metaphysical fire of inspiration, passion, ambition, and curiosity. He will speak of all these things without hesitation. He will caution you to respect fire, use it cautiously, and honor its destructive force. He speaks passionately and animatedly and tends to strike a casual tone with the magician. He will often act as a catalyst for the magician's personal goals, ever encouraging one to pursue new avenues of exploration.

The ninth eidolon often appears as a tall man sculpted entirely out of obsidian with burning eyes of fire, obsidian horns like those of an ibex, and a hairlike mane of gypsum or selenite. He dresses in a bright crimson garment that covers him from his waist to his ankles, and he is adorned with a wide necklace of gold and ruby. His sigil is the brazier, and he can be called by the cycle of flame or the burning branch.

Listening for the Ninth Eidolon

I recommend caution when attempting to contact the ninth eidolon. He is a creature of fire, and fire is what calls to him. Remember that all physical trappings are not necessary—they are just possible enhancements—so do not attempt to incorporate fire into your ritual unless you are absolutely sure you can do so safely. If you can, a campfire or bonfire is ideal to attempt your first contact ritual and meditate on this eidolon's seal while nearby. Alternatively, a safely lit candle is also a reliable aide.

Meditating while gazing into a candle is the chief way to encourage first contact from the ninth eidolon. The movements of flame are the primary mediums through which the ninth eidolon will seek to make his presence known, and that presence is often a fiery upwelling of passion to go forth and do and to be active in manifesting your goals and aspirations. Often a physical restlessness that causes a need for exercise or a hunger for hearty food can also come along with the first messages of the ninth eidolon.

The Tenth Eidolon

The tenth eidolon, the two who are one, is a celestial pairing representing the balance of opposite forces. When they appear in any humanoid approximations, one twin appears to be made of darkness and the other of light. More often they appear as shadows and reflections, as patterns of light and darkness cast upon the surfaces around the magician. These patterns are often moving and playing out their own vignettes, which are related or not to the current interaction.

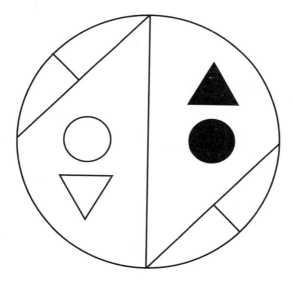

Seal of the Tenth Eidolon

The tenth eidolon holds dominion over reflections, facsimiles, illusions, and the contrast of light and darkness. Photography falls into their purview, as does projection and other forms of art where the interplay of light and shadow is the chief medium. On an inner level, the tenth eidolon is able to assist in peering into your own personal contradictions and can assist in achieving equilibrium between conflicting ideas or urges.

Like most celestials, the tenth eidolon is a creature of good will; however, they are often credited with generating more questions than answers. They can be great companions in self exploration and understanding subtle inner patterns, though. They are also capable of communicating vast conceptual underpinnings of complex facets of existence in a unique manner. They do this in a way that is much like a projection, only it is everywhere at once. It runs through you and over you, projecting images and emotions and ideas and sensations. It projects lifetimes over your consciousness to fully transmit the smallest grain of true understanding.

The tenth eidolon can be called by the two who are one, the gaze behind the mirror, or the weaving of light and shadow. Their sigil is the mirror.

Listening for the Tenth Eidolon

When contacting the tenth eidolon for the first time, it can be beneficial to stand between two mirrors, each with this eidolon's seal painted upon them. Paint one in white and one in black. It is also excellent to create an area of starkly contrasting illumination in such a way as one side of the room is dark and the other light. You can perhaps do this through use of a projector, but this can be difficult to achieve.

The tenth eidolon often communicates in the shifting of light and shadow, and they are fond of making their presence known at dusk and dawn and even in anomalies that present themselves in photographs or slides. Any interplay of reflection or shadow, trick of focus, or glint of refraction can elicit the feeling of the tenth eidolon's presence. Like many celestial eidolons, their presence is a feeling of illumination. It is like a shaft of light has been bifurcated, and one half of your being is in cool darkness while the other is bathed in warm, bright light like that of an incandescent bulb.

The tenth eidolon is also, like many celestials, enabled to communicate when you are acting in line with the aspirations of your higher self. What is unique to them, however, is that they are also eager to communicate and assist when you are experiencing times of inner conflict, especially crises of identity or other self-definition.

The Eleventh Eidolon

The eleventh eidolon is an otherworld spirit who presides over tombs and burial spaces. They are concerned with keeping the sanctity of these spaces and assuring they remain inviolate. They can grant protection and passage through places sacred to the dead for those who enter them with respect and reverence.

Seal of the Eleventh Eidolon

The eleventh eidolon can assist in funerary rites, prayers for the departed, preparation of offerings for ancestors, and helping to consecrate a space for enshrining the dead. In another capacity, they preside over natural caverns and depths within the earth, which they regard as transitory spaces between this world and various underworld dimensions. They can be called upon to protect those who enter such spaces as long as they maintain respect for the area, and as such, they can be seen as a guardian of spelunkers, archaeologists, and others whose pursuits may intersect with the resting places of the dead or deep underground areas.

The eleventh eidolon is a level and methodical, stoic presence, and their appearance varies widely, usually taking on visual aspects from the magician's culture associated with psychopomps or messengers from the afterlife. For my part, the eleventh eidolon has most often appeared to me as a skeletal figure in saffron-colored robes wielding a crude scythe of driftwood and mammoth tusk.

The eleventh eidolon, as a protector of burial places, is swift to denounce and chastise those who defile or desecrate burial chambers of the recently dead. They classify ancient burial sites as monuments, but such places do not hold the same inviolability to them as recent graves. This is due to how the eleventh eidolon views the cycle of life. In their view, only the grave of a consciousness's most recent incarnation is sacred. A grave from three lifetimes ago is to be respected, but it is no longer sacrosanct. If a consciousness transcends material incarnation, their last grave is only sacred for the span of a human lifetime. The eleventh eidolon is a nuanced enough intelligence to understand the pursuits of archaeology and does not see such as disrespectful as long as it is practiced with reverence rather than antiquarian plunder, and in some cases, they will encourage such pursuits so that people may learn of ancient funerary traditions and keep their memory alive.

The sigil of the eleventh eidolon is a small bone, easily drawn on paper, and they can be called by the yawning cavern, the sanctified tomb, or the honored headstone.

Listening for the Eleventh Eidolon

When first meditating on the seal of the eleventh eidolon, it will benefit you to do so in a place of funerary significance (if such can be done respectfully). Alternatively, a cave that you are sure is safe could work well too. A sitting area in a cemetery, somewhere near an in-home shrine for a loved one, or in a well-monitored cave in a state or national park could all enhance the meditation. While at home, burning funerary incense or keeping a book of funerary rites or a piece of rock from a cave in your circle could all benefit your contact.

The eleventh eidolon often communicates in visions of deep allegorical significance, specifically visions where they will appear and guide the magician through various places and direct their attention to symbolic vignettes that play out before them. They are also nearly always utterly silent, communicating in gestures and direct transmission of thought. They can be encouraged to make their presence known by engaging in acts of respect for the dead, such as keeping a shrine, tending a grave site, lighting candles for the dead, or attending a memorial. Their presence will often manifest as a sense of comfort, like a blanket being draped over the shoulders by a grandparent, and often this feeling will be followed by a dream journey when you next sleep. Unlike other eidolons, who will begin to converse with you in a more direct fashion, the eleventh eidolon almost always communicates cryptically.

The Twelfth Eidolon

The twelfth eidolon, whose title is the Oak King, is an otherworld spirit who holds dominion over forests and other wooded areas. He is a laughing divinity who is accompanied by stags and whose audiences are lit by dappled sunlight through high branches. His sigil is the oak leaf, and he represents both the bounty of the forest and the majesty of unspoiled places. In our inner world, he symbolizes growth, fullness, and vitality.

Seal of the Twelfth Eidolon

The twelfth eidolon is a patron of foresters, campers, hikers, arborists, and all who enter the wilderness with respect and reverence for its many wonders. He can aid one in keeping rescued animals and understanding their nonverbal cues and moods. He is fiercely protective of wild places and is unwilling to work with those who despoil them. The Oak King most often appears as a smiling human figure clad in brown and green with stag antlers.

Aside from assisting in matters of literal growth and forestry, the twelfth eidolon can help us to nurture beneficial qualities in ourselves, grow internally, and tend to the various goals and ambitions we plant in our own lives.

The twelfth eidolon is able to help us rekindle our connections to the natural world, helping us understand the earth cycle of which we are a part and engendering in us the ability to recognize the beauty of the wild. He can be called by the oaken grove or the boundless wilds.

Listening for the Twelfth Eidolon

When meditating on the seal of the twelfth eidolon, you can encourage contact by doing so while in a forest or while keeping tree leaves and naturally shed deer antlers in your circle. The twelfth eidolon will make his presence known through the movements of nature, such as the appearance of animals, the sound of wind in the trees, and the scent of leaves and loam. While observing something along these lines, you will feel his presence upon you as a welling up of appreciation for nature and a feeling of connection to the natural world from whence all came.

The twelfth eidolon can be encouraged to answer your call by engaging in outdoor activities that respect the land, such as sustainable gardening, hiking, camping in a way that leaves the land unharmed, canoeing, bird watching, or wildlife photography. He is especially fond of efforts to rehabilitate land or wildlife that have suffered through human intervention and will often respond to a request for contact immediately upon witnessing such efforts on the part of the magician.

The Thirteenth Eidolon

The thirteenth eidolon, whose title is the Bog Mother, is an otherworld spirit and sister to the twelfth eidolon. She presides over fen, swamp, and the primordial forces of birth and decay. She is the master of alga, moss, and mushroom, and in the peaty waters of her domain, biological life is originated and, in due season, returns to the cycle.

Seal of the Thirteenth Eidolon

The thirteenth eidolon excels in helping us to understand when to move on from patterns that no longer serve us and when to create new things, which we then hand over to her brother, the twelfth eidolon, to grow until they again return to her to be put to rest. She is mysterious and severe, kind to those in need and cruel to those who knowingly do harm. Hers is an ancient and primordial consciousness capable of comprehending the great ovoid cycles of existence.

The thirteenth eidolon is the mistress of metamorphosis, stewarding the mothlike mystery of complete transformation of self. She teaches us that we weave ourselves into existence and should allow no external force to define us or place us into a predetermined box. She encourages self-definition and growth, perennially emerging from the chrysalises of our past selves and spreading our wings as newer, wiser beings. This is not only applicable in a cycle of incarnation but in our daily lives as we grow and blossom into new skills, new knowledge, and new identities.

The thirteenth eidolon's sigil is the ginkgo leaf, and she often appears as a woman rising from the swamp with moss and lichen covering her like a gown and attended by alligators, turtles, and fish.

Listening for the Thirteenth Eidolon

The thirteenth eidolon is best contacted in a swamp (if such can be done safely). If not, keeping bog-native plants and vessels of water in your circle while requesting contact can also be beneficial. She is also fond of the inclusion of eggshells and bones, especially fish and reptile bones, if such can be ethically sourced through finding them in the wild.

The thirteenth eidolon is likely to make contact when you are engaged in work of personal metamorphosis, or the work of creating new things in life or removing things that no longer serve you. This can be as commonplace as building a piece of furniture or as profound as going through a transformation of core identity. Her presence can be felt as a steady gaze, mysterious and inscrutable, capable of alternating between severity and gentleness.

The Fourteenth Eidolon

The fourteenth eidolon is an otherworld spirit who presides over the manipulation of electricity, magnetism, and other invisible forces of the physical world. He is a caller of lightning and a student of subtle, immaterial sciences. He is a patron of engineers, physicists, and electricians.

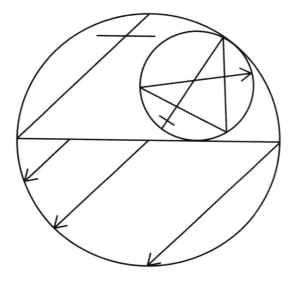

Seal of the Fourteenth Eidolon

The fourteenth eidolon aids in fostering intuition in his capacity as a master of unseen signals. He is a radio enthusiast, creature of experimentation, and companion to those who seek to study wave harmonics, signal technologies, and trans-spatial paradigms. The fourteenth eidolon delights in helping one understand how the physical and energetic worlds work, especially in aiding one to push the boundaries of our current ability to model the laws of these worlds.

On an internal level, the fourteenth eidolon is exceedingly skilled at allowing the magician to assess their own preconceived notions and hypotheses and move on from those that have been disproven, outmoded, outgrown, or are nonevidential.

The fourteenth eidolon often appears as a pulsing wave pattern of light that fluctuates in time with his voice. His sigil is the copper loop or a jagged line through a circle drawn on paper.

Listening for the Fourteenth Eidolon

The fourteenth eidolon presents a challenge for encouraging contact in your initial meditation because he does not have many physical objects that offer symbolic significance to him. It may be beneficial to a cursory degree to keep a set of magnets, a spool of copper wire, or a text pertaining to physics or electrical engineering within your circle in your first meditation.

The fourteenth eidolon can be encouraged to make contact in the days or weeks following your initial request by engaging with the subjects he enjoys through books or exercises. In addition, he can be encouraged through creating or repairing electronic devices, especially radios, or through spending time in meditation, evaluating your preconceived beliefs and assuring they stand up to the test of your current knowledge and available evidentiary materials. He will often make his presence known through a feeling such as a tingling sensation upon your consciousness and will often deliver messages in Boolean values such as yes/no or true/false.

The Fifteenth Eidolon

Iron is sacred to the fifteenth eidolon, whose sigil is two parallel vertical lines drawn inside a square, mimicking a barred window. It is a primal who understands deeply the art of binding things and the art of escaping such bondage. It is an opener of unseen doors through subtle sleight of hand. It can aid one in binding evils where they cannot do harm and releasing things kept unjustly ensnared.

Seal of the Fifteenth Eidolon

The fifteenth eidolon is skilled at helping one unwind repressed memories and unpack traumas from the past, but one must be beyond sure they are ready for such things before eliciting its help. It is also excellent at helping to make things stick, whether those are intentions, habits, or practices.

The fifteenth eidolon is equally proficient at binding ill will to a place where it cannot do harm, such as in the binding of negative vestiges (a concept elaborated on later) to items that can then be cleansed safely in a more convenient location. It is invested with particular competence in creating binding boxes in which vestiges become entangled, operating on a similar principal to Mesopotamian incantation bowls. These energy cubes attract and occupy vestiges on their own and are useful tools in advanced cleansing of burdened spaces.

The fifteenth eidolon often appears as a floating, constantly shifting ball of chains wrapped around several iron bars; it is a shape vaguely reminiscent of a spherical sea urchin. It can be called by the iron cage or the lucky lockpick.

Listening for the Fifteenth Eidolon

The fifteenth eidolon can be encouraged to respond to your request for contact when your meditation on its seal takes place with an iron bar placed at each cardinal direction of your circle. In addition, or alternatively, keeping a broken or intact lockpick in your circle, or a short length of metal chain, can also be effective as an amplifier.

The fifteenth eidolon is likely to make its presence known when you are engaged in binding work or when you are attempting to undo gates, a concept you will read of in chapter 8, that no longer serve or have begun to constrict. It is also keen to observe practices of lockpicking and locksmithing, but please make sure you are only picking locks you own. Its presence is often interesting. It is often a feeling as if you are standing in an iron cell with the door open or have a cool chain draped over your shoulders. It is not a comforting presence, but it is not a hostile one. The touch of its consciousness feels much like the moment when you sit down at a workbench with a job to do. Tools are infinitely useful, but they must be handled properly.

The Sixteenth Eidolon

The sixteenth eidolon is a primal elder statesman. His sigil, the manacle, represents the metaphorical connection that is a social order or contractual relationship, and his talents lie in marshaling vestiges and other spirit forms and serving as a negotiator and broker between parties. He is notable among primal eidolons for his vastly more flexible outlook; however, he is categorized as such for the rigid quality of his energetic presence. He is singularly programmed, but that program is diplomatic in nature.

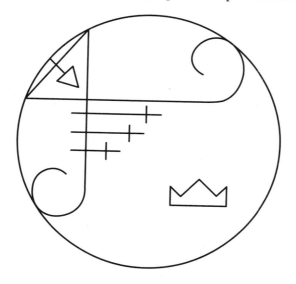

Seal of the Sixteenth Eidolon

The sixteenth eidolon can be of service in learning to speak diplomatically, mastering matters of etiquette, and understanding tactics of negotiation. He can also serve as a go-between when attempting to communicate with eidolons that are foreign to you or seem difficult to communicate with on human terms.

The sixteenth eidolon appears as a politician or diplomat, and this appearance can vary widely depending on the magician he is appearing to. For my part, he has appeared to me as a Roman senator and a Persian vizier. He is most concerned with playing out his own role as flawlessly as possible, rather than the outcomes for other involved parties, and as such, he is perhaps a bit unpredictable while at the same time quite impartial.

The sixteenth eidolon can be called by the sheaf of parchment, the lectern, or the clay tablet.

Listening for the Sixteenth Eidolon

If it were possible, the sixteenth eidolon would likely be best contacted in a municipal or government building. However, the likelihood of being able to enact a ritual meditation to request first contact in such a place is slim. Another enhancement can be found in including trappings of legal and governmental systems into your circle, using perhaps a gavel, a book on diplomacy or law, or even a lectern.

The sixteenth eidolon is often of a mind to send signals of his presence when you are engaged in some form of negotiation, legal endeavor, or business venture. His presence may be felt in the fall of a gavel, the sound of pen on paper or the click of a keyboard, or the echoes of heated discourse. His proximity gives one a feeling of gravitas and decorum, as if they have stepped suddenly into a board room, courthouse, or debate floor.

The Seventeenth Eidolon

The seventeenth eidolon holds the title of grand surveyor. It is the celestial that holds dominion over geometry, mathematics, and, most specifically, the way in which these things govern physical matter in space. It knows the height of every mountain and the volume of every pebble, and it both represents and possesses raw mathematical omniscience.

Seal of the Seventeenth Eidolon

The seventeenth eidolon understands the proportional rules of existence, the golden ratio, and the infinitely expanding universality within the tetractys. It can assist in matters of sacred geometry and in endeavors of spatial precision and drafting. It can help foster personal spatial awareness, as well as an understanding of the cosmic scale and its incalculable vastness.

The seventeenth eidolon can be difficult to communicate with linguistically. I would posit that it would be most comfortable speaking in machine code or algorithmically given its proclivities. However, as a celestial, it is more than capable of making its meaning known to the magician. It can also serve, in the same manner as all celestials, to assist in expanding overall awareness and exploring the essential qualities of existence.

The seventeenth eidolon can be called by the exponential spiral, and its sigil is the hand square or protractor.

Listening for the Seventeenth Eidolon

The seventeenth eidolon has no particular place where it may be beneficial to meditate on its sigil for first contact. All places in the physical realm contain dimensionality and measurement, and as such, they are observed and understood by the seventeenth eidolon. In order to help establish receptivity in your own mind, however, it may be beneficial to keep geometric implements in your circle, such as a hand square, protractor, ruler, or representations of the platonic solids.

The seventeenth eidolon is perhaps the easiest to encourage to respond to your request for contact through your actions. Celestials are receptive in general, and this one only needs you to exist in physical space to be encouraged. As with all celestials, acting in alignment with your higher aspirational self will also serve to encourage an answer to your first attempts at contact. For the seventeenth eidolon specifically, it can be further encouraged through acts that show mastery of your motion through physical space, such as dance, yoga, or martial arts. It also responds positively to drafting, 3D modeling, and object-oriented programming.

The Eighteenth Eidolon

The radiant one; many eyed and many winged; the unbroken circle; effulgent being of just action and just thought. This is the eighteenth eidolon, final eidolon of the inner host and gatekeeper to realms beyond. It/he/she is a celestial creature of immense power who possesses a clarity of purpose unmatched in most other intelligences.

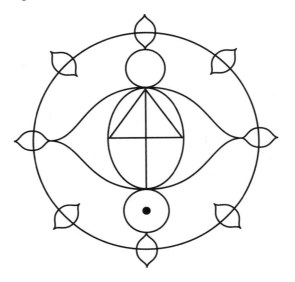

Seal of the Eighteenth Eidolon

The eighteenth eidolon seeks to eradicate suffering and sow compassionate justice in all places its/his/her gaze may fall. It/he/she is an immense force for good and a powerful beacon of hope for those lost in the twilit desert of despair that is this vale of tears. The eighteenth eidolon can help us reside in a place of righteousness, a state in which we speak only benedictions and enact only justice.

The eighteenth eidolon is a natural aid in fostering a mindset in which we seek to liberate others from exploitation, destroy systems of oppression, and lift the voices of the downtrodden. It/he/she is a righteous flame of golden light and is a boon addition to any convocation (a concept to be discussed in chapter 8) for its/his/her ability to ensure it only acts toward the highest possible good.

The eighteenth eidolon appears most often as an unbroken ring of white light around and within which many eyes of golden fire blink into and out of view. Shimmering from the edges of the ring, many sparkling wings in the hue of rainbow moonstone shift into and out of the visible spectrum as they unfurl. Geometric patterns of incomprehensible complexity trace through the air and fade away in this eidolon's vicinity.

The eighteenth eidolon can be called by the word which ends all injustice. Its/his/her sigil is the outline of an eye without cornea or pupil.

The radiance of the eighteenth eidolon is like a pool in which all selfishness, cruelty, hatred, and other behaviors that do not resonate with the unity of divine compassion will dissolve. As such, it is necessary to have done much internal work in order to contact the eighteenth eidolon. If it/he/she detects that you are not operating from a place of highest compassion, it/he/she will not appear to you. This behavior on its/his/her part is itself an exercise of mercy, for they know that if they were to reveal themselves to someone who still harbors qualities unaligned with existential harmony, it would be difficult for that person. Being forcibly shifted to a vibrational frequency for which you are not yet ready can be a disorienting experience.

Listening for the Eighteenth Eidolon

Contacting the eighteenth eidolon is not aided by any physical location or symbolic reagent. Rather, you must attempt to reside in a place within your heart where you seek to live justly and compassionately in unified harmony with all other sentient beings. To reside here, one must eschew personal ego and endeavor to dissolve into infinite compassion. Once again, this is an encouragement, not a necessity. Few of us have achieved such a state in a sustained form. It is only necessary that you are trying.

The eighteenth eidolon is likely to reach out when it/he/she believes the magician is trying sincerely to act in the interests of justice, not as defined by any fallible, fleeting mortal code or court but by the singular law of the harmonious unity of consciousness. Only when the magician holds a sincere desire to live from a place of compassion, with service of others held above service of self, can sustained communication with the eighteenth eidolon occur. This is not to say that the eighteenth eidolon will only communicate with fully realized paragons of virtue, ascended masters, and bodhisattvas, but it will only communicate with those who hold such ascension as an aspiration. As such, those who aspire to harm or selfishness will be unable to sustain enduring communication with the eighteenth eidolon, and as such, they will be unable to progress beyond the octadecagon gate, which marks the threshold of the deepest work.

Utilizing Eidolon Entries

Having read through the entries of the eighteen eidolons of the inner host of the ark, you are now ready to begin to work with them. This is done, as described earlier in this chapter, by meditating on their seals and listening for signs they may send you in the days and weeks beyond your initial attempt at contact. I advise you to engage in this practice with at least three eidolons before proceeding further in this book. Once you have received names from at least three eidolons, you will be ready to engage in the practices to follow.

Working effectively with eidolons takes time. You will need to learn to understand when one is attempting to communicate, learn to differentiate between the nuanced signs sent by the eidolons you know, and learn the personalities and preferences of each you wish to work with. Eventually, you will reach the point where you can have full-fledged conversations with eidolons at the same level of detail you would with a physically present friend. I urge you to treat eidolons with respect. They exist on a wavelength we cannot fully comprehend and have access to insights we would be hard pressed to interpret on our own. Eidolons are meant to be advisers, counselors, and even colleagues. They are meant to be worked alongside of, not to serve or be served. Eschew the idea of transaction or hierarchy when approaching eidolons.

Once you have made successful, lasting contact with at least three of the inner host, you are ready to take the next step forward in your journey. Up until this point you will have worked with eidolons previously known to you through this book. Moving forward you will learn to discover new eidolons through the process of illumination. In order to do this, a symbolic threshold ritual is provided. Just as the Circle of Concentric Ascension serves as a statement of intention to work as a magician and communicate with eidolon intelligences, so does the following ritual, the Passage of the Octadecagon Gate, serve as a statement of intention to open yourself to the detection of new eidolons as yet to be discovered. Once this ritual is completed, you will be ready to move to further chapters in which you will discover how to deepen your meditative focus, create a sacred thought-space for the manifestation of your work, and illuminate new eidolons.

The Passage of the Octadecagon Gate

The octadecagon gate is the threshold through which all eidolons beyond the inner host wait. It is possible to have a fulfilling and engaging lifetime of magic without ever passing beyond it—both in other systems and even in this one. Indeed, you could simply work with a few eidolons of the inner host for the rest of your magical exploration and do meaningful and fulfilling work. It is, however, my recommendation that all magicians pursuing the practice of paneidolism attempt to pass the octadecagon gate so that they may begin to illuminate new eidolons.

The octadecagon gate is kept by the eighteenth eidolon. In order to pass through it, you must display to the eidolon your intentions to use your magic for compassionate ends. This can be seen in an external paradigm as being granted access to an actual wavelength of existence into which you have not previously been initiated. Alternatively, in an internal paradigm, it may be seen as unlocking a wellspring of inner potential through achieving a clarity of purpose. No matter the way in which you may look at it, it is the doorway to illuminating new eidolons.

Let me be clear: one can meet new eidolons without having passed the octadecagon gate. However, the efficacy and frequency of doing so is greatly increased if this ritual is enacted. Passing the octadecagon gate is as lighting a torch in your consciousness through which beneficent eidolons are attracted, seeking to manifest the concepts with which they resonate into the density of the material world.

As with most of the rituals I have acquainted you with, there are few physical reagents involved in the Passage of the Octadecagon Gate. There is, however, a bit of prework involved. In order to embark through the octadecagon gate, you must approach through one of two avenues. The first angle of approach is to contact three eidolons, have a working rapport, and have each agree to vouch for you in this ritual. The second avenue is to work directly with the eighteenth eidolon for a month or so and ask for its own judgment on your passage. I will cover both options where they are relevant in the details of the ritual to follow.

To begin with, you will require your scepter of art; whether your scepter of artifice is used to house it is entirely to your preference. You will also need the seal of the eighteenth eidolon on paper or drawn upon the ground in front of you. Rather than simply drawn on its own, it should be drawn within a square to represent the boundary lines of a door. In addition, a smaller circle should be drawn on the top, left, and right of the square. Leave the bottom of the square, facing you where you are standing, without a smaller circle. If you are calling upon three eidolons to vouch for your passage, you will draw each of their sigils in the three small circles. If you are relying on the eighteenth eidolon to judge your passage alone, you will draw a single eye outline with a key within it in each of these circles.

Begin by using your preferred space-setting ritual. Then you will stand at or focus on the base of the square, facing the seal of the eighteenth eidolon within it and the sigils, or eye-keys, to the left, right and above it. You will hold your scepter above your head with your dominant hand, beginning with your head bowed and your open nondominant hand down at your side, palm facing forward.

There are two paths forward on the flow chart of this ritual: one in which you are calling three eidolons to vouch for your passage, and one in which you are relying on an existing rapport with the eighteenth eidolon to bring you across the threshold. If you are engaging in the former path, you will begin by calling the three eidolons that have agreed to vouch for you. Which eidolons you have spoken with will be up to you, but the general idea for their call follows. Keep in mind that you can change this language in the way that feels best to you, as long as it consists of calling the eidolons and stating the purpose for doing so in this ritual.

An example for this purpose is as follows:
"{Name and titles or epithets of the eidolon you have selected}, I call you by the {call phrase of the eidolon you have selected} to bear witness to my passage through the octadecagon gate. Vouchsafe your guidance and commendation upon me that I may walk under the eyes of the eighteenth eidolon and be found in harmony with the omniscient multiverse."

Say this, or something like this, when focusing upon each of the outer sigils in turn for each eidolon thereby represented.

If you have chosen to gain passage through the eighteenth eidolon, you will eschew the need for invoking three other eidolons and will, instead, invoke the eighteenth eidolon three times, each time affirming your desire to work in harmony with the rhythmic dance of existence. Starting with the leftmost eye-key symbol, say the following three affirmations, or something like them, passing to the next eye-key with each invocation.

At the first eye-key:
"{Name and titles or epithets of the eighteenth eidolon}, who stands at the fulcrum of the scale, who sees all in harmony and discord, by the word which ends all injustice I call your gaze to me. Witness my approach of the octadecagon gate in the spirit of service to all that vibrates with the harmony of existence."

At the next eye-key:
"{Name and titles or epithets of the eighteenth eidolon}, who stands at the hub of the wheel, who sees all in harmony and discord, by the word which ends all injustice I call your gaze to me. Witness the hope of my will before the threshold of the octadecagon gate in the desire to seed kindness in endless realities."

At the final eye-key:
"{Name and titles or epithets of the eighteenth eidolon}, who refracts through existence like light through a prism, who sees all in harmony

and discord, by the word which ends all injustice I call your gaze to me. Witness the hand of my will upon the keystone of the octadecagon gate in the desire to pass beyond."

At this juncture, whether you have arrived via three recommendations or three invocations of the eighteenth eidolon, you will proceed in the same manner.

Raise your head from the bowed position, focus your attention on the center of the eighteenth eidolon's seal before you, and bring your scepter to rest upon the center of your chest. Then bring your opposite hand to rest over it. You will now speak the following words, or something in your own words stating a similar sentiment:

"I stand ready to receive the messages of the eidolons beyond the inner host, that we may work together for mutual and universal benefit and proliferate harmony in the song of existence. I stand ready to emanate with justice and compassion, in unity with the totality of sentience and free from avarice, cruelty, or hatred. I stand at the doorway, the threshold between all that I have been and all that I may yet be, beneath the innumerable eyes of the eighteenth eidolon, and I seek passage."

After this statement, unclasp your hands and use your scepter to tap three times on each of the sigils or eye-keys, and then nine times in the center of the seal of the eighteenth eidolon. This is a symbolic knocking upon the octadecagon gate. From here, the body of the ritual is complete. You may receive a direct and immediate sign that you have been granted passage, a sudden broadening of sensory awareness, a vision, or a strong feeling. On the other hand, you may not, and this is also fine. You may come gradually into awareness of the answer of the eighteenth eidolon.

After the symbolic knocking on the doorway, you can begin to wrap up the ritual. The first step, if you have invoked three eidolons, is to thank the eidolons involved for their time and attention to your work, as is courteous. You may do so in whatever words you desire, or by using the following phrase:

"Eidolons who have vouchsafed my passage, I thank you for your partnership in this endeavor. I bid you good will and dissolve now the outer sigils which called you to this work, go in peace."

If you did not invoke three eidolons and instead beseeched the eighteenth eidolon three times, you may wish to simply thank the eighteenth eidolon as you see fit, or by using the following phrase:

"{Name and titles or epithets of the eighteenth eidolon}, who keeps the octadecagon gate of the outer host, I part from you under the gaze of your illuminant eyes. I thank you for this chance at passage. Should I pass through the gate ahead I do so with gratitude. If I cannot yet complete the voyage, I will return without ill will when next I attempt it."

Now you may sit for a time in the ritual consciousness before closing your circle and uttering your closing phrase, or "So it is," if you do not have another you prefer.

Chapter 6
MAINTAINING AND EXPANDING YOUR PRACTICE

Now that you have drunk deeply of this book, having contacted at least three eidolons and attempted the Passage of the Octadecagon Gate, you have established a functioning practice. Do not grow complacent now that you have arrived at this point. Every day is an opportunity to further your connections with the eidolons you know and forge new ones with eidolons you've yet to discover. Furthermore, you may now begin to develop ways to apply your relationships with these eidolons to myriad facets of your life.

Having manifested through action the foundations of your practice in the preceding chapters, the following chapters will build upon that foundation. In this chapter, we will discuss techniques and concepts meant to aid you in both maintaining your existing practice and growing and developing your practice to suit your unique personal vision. In the chapter after, we will touch on tools for developing your own techniques and rituals that are meant to foster a lifetime of esoteric discovery. Finally, we will conclude this second half of our time together by discussing advanced techniques meant to offer transformative options for your practice if you should wish to explore them.

Deepening Your Meditative Foundation

One of the pillars of our practice is endeavoring to maintain a meditative state. As you progress, you should ideally be meditating daily. The various obligations of life can make this difficult, and you should not be discouraged if your meditation is by necessity more sporadic. However, daily, or even more frequent, meditation should be the goal to aspire to. Meditation clears the mind of all the worldly clutter that assails it daily in the commotion of human society. This need not be a daunting task, as meditation can manifest in many ways. While formal seated meditation with visualization and deep breath exercises is essential (and you should avail yourself of it as often as possible), the heart of meditation is to become aware. You can achieve awareness on the subway, at a restaurant, at work, or anywhere, really. Through meditation we can realize that time itself is illusory, and a moment of true awareness is as profound as an hour or a lifetime. Eventually we can learn to maintain our awareness through all of life.

Meditation is not a thing you do but a state you maintain, and it can be maintained while chopping wood as proficiently as when sitting upon a cushion. When we are aware, we understand that we are not our body or our thoughts. We understand that all things are impermanent save consciousness and that consciousness is the act of perceiving, of being, and of experiencing. Too often we associate consciousness with analyzing, deducing, worrying, and identifying. Consciousness, that which pervades, requires only abiding in each moment, noting all that we perceive and allowing those perceptions to pass. Thoughts are like leaves in the wind that we must watch as they pass rather than chase to our ruin. Presence is the goal.

One of the key things to perceive and be present for, to feel the flow of, is energy. The thought energy of existence can, at times, be felt like a great ringing. It is like a high, clear tone that comes at once from all things. All of existence is pulsating with radiance if we but allow ourselves to abide and witness it. In deep meditation we can also feel and expand the energy flowing through our own physical bodies—the anchor points for our consciousness in this world. We visualize this flow in the Middle Pillar Exercise and the Rigpa and White Thread Meditations. Visualizing in this manner will allow us to internalize that flow and understand when it changes due to any form of perturbation of self, which should in turn call us back to meditation to reenforce that flow. In understanding what it feels like to be centered and aware, we can also understand what it feels like to lose that state and thus focus on reestablishing it. This will also allow us to grow in our capacity for our great work of magic; it keeps us from getting stuck in a nonreceptive state.

Transitioning from meditation as a thing we do to a way we live allows us to also listen for the presence of eidolons, whose proximity is often most readily detectable through fluctuations in the energy around us. Once we detect new eidolons, it is beneficial to have a dedicated space to receive their seals. This is a thought-space unbound by physical geography, and we call it a temple of mind.

Building a Temple of Mind

Now that you have focused on cultivating your meditative practice further, you will combine that faculty with the visualization skills fostered throughout this book. You have consecrated space, set boundaries, and given respect to points beyond. These skills are also useful when you are not in the ritual circle. Specifically, they will aid you in the construction of your temple of mind.

A temple of mind is a visualized thought construct. It is a conceptual space for you to meditate that serves as a theater for visions, a foyer for the reception of nonphysical guests, and a parlor in which you may relax and abide in peace. Perhaps it contains all these rooms, or perhaps it is a small shrine on a high mountain that serves all these purposes. Its form is yours to discover and create.

You will begin to architect your temple of mind in meditation. As you sit or stand in meditation, eyes closed and body relaxed, set your intention to establish a realm of your own, and reach out with your senses. At first you will visualize only darkness before you begin to awaken each of the senses to the realm around you.

You will begin with the sensation of touch. What surface are you standing or sitting upon? Is it rough or smooth? Does it give, or is it unyielding?

Do your feel cool marble or sun-warmed moss? Further, is there wind on your face, or is there rain falling upon you? Do leaves dance around you, brushing against your body? What is it that springs to mind as you begin to visualize the tactile sensations of your own inner temple?

Moving forward, what scents are around you? Do you detect aromatic incense in the air or the scent of flowers? Perhaps the dusty smell of old books clings to the space surrounding you. Breathe deeply and visualize what enters your awareness as you construct the temple around you.

Proceeding, what sounds surround you? The rustling of branches? The chiming of bells? The calling of birds? Do curtains rustle in the breeze or rains pound upon the roof? What ambient noises, if any, does your realm play host to?

Finally, you will begin to visualize sight with your mind's eye. Though your physical eyes remain closed, you will open the eye of visualization to view the realm around you. What has produced the feelings, scents, and sounds that surround you? Rouse yourself in mind, while your physical body remains still, from your resting pose and begin to traverse your space. This first area you find yourself in is your sanctum. It is the area in which you may repose and contemplate without interruption. Is it a structure, a natural formation, or perhaps even a vehicle? Run your hands over its surfaces and note its adornments.

Continuing, you will survey your realm—your temple of mind—area by area. Its breadth and detail are completely yours to survey. Perhaps your realm is a castle of many rooms adorned with arcane carvings and smelling of old vellum and ink. Perhaps it is a garden on a high cliff overlooking an ocean, containing but a single overgrown chair. Your temple can be anything, and you can reform, readorn, edit, and rebuild it at your leisure. What is important is that you understand it is a sacred space for you. It is a place to organize your intentions and enact the simple daily matters of magic you will encounter. This temple of mind is the place in which you will forge your emblems, which is an important task in the daily work of a paneidolist magician that you will learn of in the next chapter.

You will want to take notes on your temple of mind, or even sketch out its various features, in your tome. Keeping a chronicle in your tome should be a step for all meditative or ritualistic observations. Your temple of mind should be as a real place to you—more real than many in the physical world in time.

Your temple of mind, like your scepter of art, is a thought construct. It can be remodeled at your will through the same meditations used to create it. It should evolve and grow as your practice grows and evolves, thus necessitating new thought-space for new ideas and techniques.

You will primarily use your temple of mind to meditate on the notions of new eidolons until their seals are revealed to you, and you will also use it as a place to visualize communication with eidolons. You will also use it for several of the techniques in the next chapter, so before we proceed you will need to learn a little about working with energy centers beyond the Middle Pillar that will be used in these exercises.

Working Beyond the Middle Pillar

Having built your temple of mind, you will soon discover practices to be enacted within it. Many of these practices will necessitate the focusing of energy into spaces or objects. Earlier in this book you learned to center the flow of energy through your body by focusing on energy centers in the middle of your form. Most energy systems identify secondary and tertiary energy centers beyond this central column. In previous exercises you have used the energy centers in your hands to charge first your prana mudra and then your scepter of art. These energy centers are some of many you may explore through your meditations and are of particular importance to the work ahead, specifically the creation of emblems. The energy centers in the palms are highly tuned projective and receptive loci. Think of them as both transmitters and receivers. They can be used to reach out and feel the flow of energy, discern its nature, and project your own intentions outward. Keep in mind that the energetic body exists on a different wavelength from the physical body, and as such, these energy centers are present even when physical hands may not be. To reiterate a core concept of this practice, the sole necessary tool is will.

Here I will present you with a meditation designed to bring your focus to the palm energy centers and daily exercises to sharpen your discernment with them. Do not neglect these exercises; they form the foundation of the next step of your practice.

Blossoming Hand Meditation

In preparation for this meditation, you should create a space of low light for yourself. This can be done by lighting a single candle placed on a safe surface and turning off the lights in the room, by dimming lights (if that feature is available to you), or by lighting a small battery-powered LED lamp in a dark room. If you are relying on natural light, you will need to perform this meditation near sunrise or sunset. You may also wish to play calming music or light incense to aid in your meditation if these notions appeal to you.

You will begin this meditation with your rhythmic breathing exercises, breathing in deeply, holding that breath for a few seconds, and exhaling slowly. As you do so, bend your arms at the elbow and hold your hands palm up. If you are seated, you may wish to rest the backs of your hands on your knees.

Begin to go through the visualizations of the Middle Pillar Exercise or the Rigpa or White Thread Meditations; choose whichever appeals to you in the moment. During the meditation you have chosen for this step, you need only perceive the energy flowing, rather than engage in the full ritual. As you abide in this flow for a few minutes, begin to feel the energy gather in your torso, suffusing your shoulders, chest, and solar plexus. As it gathers, envision it pulsating and then flowing from your torso, over your shoulders and down your arms, into the palms of your hands. Resonate in this flow for a while, feeling the energy of existence flow through your chest and down your arms, beginning to gather in the palms of your hands.

As the minutes pass, begin to feel the energy gathering in your hands coalesce into a sphere of white light in each palm. As these spheres grow to fill the center of your palms, feel them begin to spin, as a gyroscope does, and emanate their own unique radiance. Feel them become clearer and more resonant.

As you continue to feel this energy coalescing, in a calm sense of focus devoid of urgency or grasping, open your eyes and gaze at your palms. In the dim light you may be able to glimpse the energy in your palms with the subtle senses that overlay your sight. Feel the pleasant intensity of the energy flowing into your palms, charging these energy centers.

After a few minutes, when you feel comfortable, begin to raise your hands in front of you. Move your hands through the space immediately before you and allow energy to flow through them, which is being drawn through the central pillar of energy that is the wellspring of magical power sent down the arms and out from the energy centers in your palms. This should induce a feeling of expansion or blossoming in your palms. Take note of what feelings, visualizations, or sensations this exercise produces for later recording in your tome.

When you feel that you are finished exploring this flow of energy through your hands, bring them down to waist height with your arms bent at the elbows, resting on them your knees if seated. Slowly close your hands into lightly clenched fists and feel the energy in your hands and arms return to a resting level, ebbing back from focused intensity to the natural flow of everyday awareness. As you do so, begin to rouse yourself from the focused state and rise from meditation.

Expanding Your Ark through the Illumination of Eidolons

Having completed the preceding three exercises in this chapter, having successfully contacted at least three eidolons, and having enacted the Passage of the Octadecagon Gate, you are now ready to begin discovering new eidolons, referred to here as illuminating them.

To illuminate eidolons, the number one skill to develop is present-moment awareness, or a state of deep listening to the world around and within you in any given moment. You have been regularly developing this skill from the very beginning through the Middle Pillar Exercise, Rigpa Meditation, and White Thread Meditation.

As you go about your day, and in your meditations, you must keep keenly aware of the possible presence of an eidolon. This is a feeling you will grow remarkably familiar with through working with those eidolons whose attention you already have. When you feel the presence of an eidolon—a tug in the periphery of your mind—enter your temple of mind, focus upon that presence, and visualize a circle. The single unbroken circle is the root of all eidolon sigils, as well as the space in which the magician's practice unfolds, and I would consider the circle to be the symbol of the practice described in this book. Pay close attention to the notions that come to you as you visualize this perfect circle; examine the feelings, words, and images. Eventually you should begin to see that circle, the outer boundary of a seal, begin to fill itself out. Once you have glimpsed the seal, you can open your eyes and step out from your temple of mind Write down the resulting seal in your tome and, when you are ready, reflect upon it in your ritual circle. It may take several meditations to successfully view the seal that you are beginning to glimpse, and for some eidolons, your success may be affected by the time of day or the environment.

Occasionally during this initial visualization process you will also hear a name clearly. If you do, this eidolon is eager to contact you, but you should still wait until you are in your circle to make first contact. It is important to be in a controlled space in which you feel safe when first contacting any new eidolons. I have yet to encounter a malevolent eidolon, but some do possess such unfiltered power that it is best to meet them where you are fully and actively grounded and centered.

Once you have begun to communicate with an eidolon, you should discover qualities about it that will eventually lead you to assign it a sigil, or a small glyph that can be drawn upon a slip of paper or engraved upon a similarly sized object. You will note this sigil in the eidolon's entry in your tome, either writing the glyph itself or describing it. During these meditations, as your communication with the eidolon becomes clearer and more coherent, you will understand enough of the eidolon's qualities to discern a call. As mentioned, all calls to eidolons follow a similar formula, which is as follows:

"{Name and/or epithet(s) of the eidolon}, I stand in a circle of my own design and call you by {phrase, concept, or thematic conceit

of importance to the eidolon}. Will you {entreat/collaborate/commune/abide} with me?"

This practice should culminate in your being able to go about your daily life and call upon eidolons for advice or assistance at a moment's notice in any situation. What began as a methodical ritual practice can be employed, once the working relationship is established with the eidolon you are contacting, as a short invocation through envisioning a circle of your own design and making use of an eidolon's sigil and call.

Sharing Illuminations

Once you have illuminated a new eidolon, there are circumstances in which you may wish to introduce that eidolon to other magicians for their benefit. While sharing an eidolon's information against that eidolon's wishes is considered a grave breach of trust and can result in loss of contact with the affronted eidolon, it can be done with an eidolon's consent. Most often an eidolon will indicate that they are open to working with other magicians and request you make known their seal. A seal is an invitation, and as such, it does not need to be answered. When a magician ruminates on an eidolon's seal, the eidolon may observe them and determine if they wish to make contact. The entirety of this book is predicated upon this foundation, and all of the eidolons included in this book have consented to their seals and general descriptions being shared with the wider world in an attempt to assist prospective adepts in their development.

Much more rarely, an eidolon may observe your interactions with someone and request you give that person their seal and sigil. Alternatively, certain eidolons are happy to talk with anyone at least once and do not mind their names being shared as well. These eidolons will make this preference known. However, a name is a phone number and not a command, so just because someone has an eidolon's name does not mean that eidolon will continue to communicate, especially if they feel an individual is not a good fit for working with them.

It is my hope that those who engage in the paneidolist system detailed in this book will find one another and work together toward their own self-betterment. As such, the sharing of illuminated eidolons should become—if not exactly common—at least not rare. With this in mind, I recommend incorporating a sheaf of sturdy card stock or unlined index cards into your working tools. Using the same pens that you employ in your tome, you may copy seals onto these cards for sharing among your fellow practitioners. It is not inappropriate to note a few characteristics on these cards, much like the eidolon entries in this book. These descriptions can vary in length and detail based upon factors such as your own depth of practice with the specified eidolon or that eidolon's willingness to share with other magicians.

Here it is also vital to note that how an eidolon appears to you may be wholly different from how they appear to another. There is no correct or incorrect interpretation of an eidolon. They are infinitely self-morphic and in some paradigms represent parts of the subconscious, so it stands that they differ as magicians differ. Tangling yourself up in codifying and policing the details of eidolons is counterproductive to the work and can drive a wedge in your working group. Every new interpretation of an eidolon is a chance to learn from one another. There is only one inviolable principal in this system, and that is to operate without harm and with compassion.

Finding a Guide

Once you have illuminated several eidolons, you will likely be at a place where you are comfortable enough with their presence and the experience of communicating with them to warrant exploring keeping a few around in a more permanent capacity than call-based interactions. The concept of guides, or familiar spirits, is an ancient one steeped in magical history. While popular culture has generally depicted this relationship as between a practitioner and an animal of some sort, the idea has historically included nonphysical beings as well. For our purposes, a guide is an eidolon with which you work closely who serves as an adviser and aide to you in your practice. Any of the eidolons of the inner host, whose seals have been specifically revealed in this book, would make wonderful guides, as they are known for their patience, wisdom, and willingness to work with new practitioners.

Working with a guide is not for everyone. Although all eidolons can be considered guides of a fashion in some ways, the idea of a dedicated guide goes somewhat beyond the instance-based interaction with most eidolons. While you may call an eidolon to help you heal from an injury or complete a difficult task, they generally do not stick around for indeterminate lengths of time. Guides, however, have carte blanche to enter your space and your life; it is part of the agreement that connects them to you. A guide needs to come when they feel they are needed, and therefore, they can come at any time. Furthermore, a guide will often even be present to help in your work with other eidolons.

In order to find a guide, it is important that you set that intention. As part of your daily meditations, project your wish to work with a guide into the universe. One useful visualization is to imagine that desire as energy flowing through your scepter to form a sphere of light at its tip. When that sphere has grown large and luminous, send it forth into the distance with a wave of your scepter. Watch it float upward like a paper lantern and disappear into the horizon.

After a few weeks of the above exercise, providing you are listening for eidolons as you now always should be, you may be contacted by a new eidolon who has answered your call for a guide.

Another route for securing a guide is to simply ask an eidolon you feel you have a good rapport with the next time you call them. It is respectful to go through a formal ritual circle when doing this, incorporating your scepter of artifice, rather than simply calling them into a circle of your own design as you normally would. Showing this extra effort, though it may not be a part of your regular practice with familiar eidolons, is courteous.

Some people find it useful to enlist many guides, while some prefer to partner with just one. Whatever you wish, just be sure that when you discuss the possibility of an eidolon being your guide you are both exceedingly clear on how you define that relationship and what is expected from each party involved.

Incorporating Eidolons into Your Life

Whether you view it as accessing your inner potential or contacting another realm, working with eidolons can generally enrich your stay on earth in myriad ways. You may think of them as helping hands, expert advisers, and allies in your corner. Incorporate them into your practices as holistically as possible, not just in magic but in all of life. Not only can they sit with you in meditation, but they can also inspire you as you cook, jog, write, paint, or even just trudge through this worldly life's many obligatory drudgeries with a modicum of optimism. They are, above all else perhaps, advisers.

At the most external view, eidolons can be viewed as extradimensional intelligences possessing insights beyond mortal ken. At the most internal view, eidolons can be viewed as personified archetypal insights into the deep subconscious mind developed through regular meditative practice. In each of these views, it is undeniably useful to foster a partnership with such thoughtforms for the insight they provide.

Learning to work with eidolons, like many things worth doing, requires practice. When you begin you may find that you perceive but glimpses of messages, like faded postcards from far away. The more you hone your skills, the more you will perceive, and eventually you may find yourself at a place where conversation flows freely and in real time. However, you may also find that, outside of ritual awareness, your messages are always cryptic or symbolic. This is fine, everyone's senses are different.

It is possible—even likely and perhaps nigh inevitable—that work with eidolons will change the way you live your life. This has to do with the fact that working with eidolons is no less than incorporating a previously unseen layer of reality into the calculations of your daily routine. It may happen gradually, or you may wake up one morning and be hit by the realization that your life is indelibly other than it once was. In some ways, the form of magic I put forth in this book is akin to hacking your consciousness. You are upgrading your awareness to detect things you could not before, and now erstwhile empty rooms may suddenly be home to energetic patterns and intelligences. A previously boring trip to the grocery store may now be host to myriad inner conversations with strange and fascinating beings. Whether these phenomena are interpreted as access to a deeper part of the subconscious or an actual outer realm will be dependent on your paradigm, but they represent a change in awareness either way.

While it is important to incorporate the existence of eidolons holistically into your life it is equally, if not more, important to assure that this does not overtake the rest of your life. This is to say that we, as magicians, are meant to stand on the fulcrum between the seen and unseen worlds and not to allow our focus to stray too far into either. We should not focus on the material world to the neglect of our magical pursuits, and we should not focus on our magic to the detriment of physical world health and relationships. A balance is to be struck. Our magic should help us be more present in the mundane world when it is appropriate, and our workaday lives should give us the time to set aside for our magic. It is no better to illuminate eidolon seals while driving than it is to text and drive. Give each task at hand its attention.

Chapter 7
LIVING AS A MAGICIAN

In the preceding chapter, you learned to expand upon your foundational practice with set techniques and concepts. In this chapter, you will learn ways to develop your own unique magical toolbox of emblems and rituals and to begin to develop a definition of your practice based upon the themes and ideas you have chosen.

This chapter is titled "Living as a Magician" because I wish to make the deliberate distinction that one does not "do" magic. Rather, one lives it; one is it. Too often the inquiring mind seeks out magic as a dabbler, thinking that magic is a tool like a rake, which can be picked up when needed and placed in a shed when no longer required for a specific task. This is not an appropriate metaphor for magic, but it is one that is easily espoused in a world where instant gratification and commodification are the cultural norms. Magic is much more like a musical instrument. It requires practice, dedication, and nuanced understanding to master. A beginner will squeak out simple melodies while a virtuoso will conjure forth symphonies seemingly from nowhere, but truly it will be from decades of dedication unseen by the audience. These are both valid positions on the musician's path—beginner and virtuoso—as long as they are both focused on improvement. There is no shame in being a beginner and no mystery to being a master. It is solely a matter of how much time and effort has been put in so far. Even this musical metaphor, however, is lacking. This is due to the fact that an instrument is not with you through every moment of your day, and magic very much is. Magic is a mindset, a wavelength, and a state of being.

The Transmutation of the Magician

Magic is one of the few schools of instruction that seeks to eschew itself at the pinnacle of its practice. Magic is meant to bring you to a transcendent state, a clarity of will, and a singularity of purpose. Once that has been achieved, magical practice is no longer strictly required. You need not engage in formal magic for you have thoroughly attuned to it to the point where you no longer perceive yourself as separate from it. This is the reason why I have emphasized that you need not be hung up on specific tools or language. These are all distractions from abiding in the flow of magic. I often say that I do not cast spells. This is to say that I have mostly eschewed the need for elaborate ritual because I do my best to abide in the state of ritual consciousness at all times. I still engage in ritual because it is a beautiful practice, especially to mark holidays or milestones, but I understand intrinsically that it is not actually necessary. As I stated early on, only will is necessary, and it can be used to direct the subtle harmonies of existence without fanfare or obscura. I do not cast spells, because I have moved beyond the need to convince myself I must create effect through elaborate means. I simply accept that the effect will come to pass as I will it when I direct that will upon the energies around me.

If you have followed the instructions in this book so far, you have likely taken copious notes on the many observations you have made while engaging in the frequent meditations and rituals prescribed. It is highly likely that you have seen and experienced things you did not expect to—things that may have challenged your prior assertions about magic and about reality in general.

Each of us dies many deaths before the mortal vessel ultimately perishes. These are ego deaths, or times when we must challenge our assertions and accept that our paradigms have changed and we must change as a result. The ego is the most insidious enemy of the magician. Pridefully refusing to abandon old assertions when new evidence is presented is to accept the entropic heat death of personal growth and, ultimately, of any true gnosis.

If you have followed this book to this point, by sheer repetitive meditation alone it has likely changed you in some way. It is difficult to spend any amount of time in silent contemplation without growth taking place. If you have followed the path to the letter, initiated yourself through concentric ascension, and spoken with eidolons, you now likely consider yourself a magician.

To be a magician is to move through mortal existence with a certain set of suppositions. These are ones you have made for yourself and developed through your practice. These hypotheses about the nature of magic and reality should always be tested and expanded as you move forward. However, regardless of your operating paradigm, you have become something you may not have been before.

To be a magician is to accept that will holds power, energy permeates existence, such energy is capable of being directed by will, and intelligences inhabit the world and the self that can be called up to realize potentiality and assist in making will manifest. The cornerstone of magic is to understand that will can be exercised to greater strength by practices of visualization and ritual, and perception of the subtle geometry of existence can be manifested and explored in the stillness of meditation. It is to recognize that all mastery begins first and foremost with self-mastery, and all harm is tantamount to self-harm.

To be a magician is to be an experimental applied ontologist. This is to say that one is always seeking to understand existential mysteries through the application of magical practices. The answers you find will change you. The road of the magician can be a lonely one; it will cause you to think along avenues that may be considered odd, taboo, or simply alien to others. To this, I must quote Euripides: "To the fool, he who speaks wisdom will sound foolish." In this age, when even physically reproducible and readily quantifiable science is often denied, certainly the subtle art of magic is difficult to explain to the uninitiated. Magic can be said to have, paradoxically, both a low and high cost of entry. Physically speaking, the art of magic can be entered into with no monetary cost at all. It simply takes a willingness to learn and an openness to the unquantifiable. However, it also requires an eschewing of vanity, a humility of spirit, and a great deal of patience for nonimmediate results gleaned through self-cultivation. These prices are exceedingly difficult for some to muster payment for.

Chasing Eternity

The further you progress in your practice of this system, the more tuned in to the motions of the indelible patterns of existence you will become. I feel it would be intellectually dishonest of me not to tell you that this will make you very odd by societal standards. Normalcy is a social construct, but it is also a mathematical one; it is a bell curve that expresses what behaviors the average member of a society will exhibit in a given situation. The average person is, perhaps unfortunately, not a magician. Therefore, the average person cannot observe the patterns that will become a large part of your decision-making processes. As such, your behavior may seem irrational to others. In order to accurately determine the rationality of a decision, a person needs to understand all factors involved. To the outside observer, who will be missing certain vital factors due to limitations in their own powers of observation, your journey from point A to point B in decision-making may seem nonsensical. To use an example, let us say it is sunny outside in the morning, but the weather report predicts rain showers in the afternoon. You decide to take an umbrella with you when you leave your home. Your neighbor sees you walking outside with an umbrella under your arm but has not seen the weather report. They think that you are odd for carrying an umbrella on such a beautiful day, because they are missing a vital piece of information. It will be as such when those who are not attuned to the rhythms of existence view the actions of those who are.

To pursue magic is to accept that you do not have the answers, that existence is messy and beautiful, and that you can spend lifetimes glimpsing the ineffable revolutions of the divine mechanism without making any neat, tidy, or comforting sense out of them. This is difficult for many people.

Forming a practice group is one way to find those with whom you can commiserate. Whether you call it by mystical epithets, such as coven, cabal, or circle, or other such terms, the general idea is the same. These are groups in which you can practice magic together or practice separately and discuss results, observations, and theories together, or some combination of the two. In this system specifically, these groups can also be formed to share or co-illuminate the seals of eidolons who have expressed interest in assisting new adepts.

It is easier today, perhaps, than ever before to form such groups because of the saturation of telecommunications technologies in our lives. We are almost always one screen away from a video conference, online forum, or social media group of like-minded individuals. Of course, there is always something to be said for old fashioned face-to-face contact through which we may share such social sacraments as a mutual meal or physical ritual.

Dedication to the art will not only likely affect your relationships, naturally causing you to both seek other magicians with whom to communicate and avoid those who live in inflexible ego-fueled paradigms, but it will also affect the way you go about your daily life. At a certain point, you will no longer have room for certain things. You will lose attachments to physicality, understanding that consciousness is unbound by the body, which serves merely as a conduit to translate it into the material world. You will lose most fear of physical death for this reason as well. The hormones of the body, adrenaline and the like, will still function, but in the calm spaces of your perception, you will understand that you are not your body.

In addition, you will have learned to take a step backward from your ego. Through meditation and discernment, you will realize that all consciousnesses are simply proceeding along the journey of incarnation at their own pace. It is neither possible to look down on someone nor envy someone for where they are on their spiritual path; you can only tend to your own path. Your path is the only one your will can control without harming others through the abrogation of their own will. You cannot tend to your garden while obsessing over your neighbor's, and the more you meddle in theirs, the further yours will fall into neglect. Rather, you may tend your garden and hope that you do so in a way that sets an example for those who wish to garden in the same manner. Similarly, you will learn not to become inflated by your successes or discouraged by your failures. These are only steps upon the path, and lingering on them impedes forward motion. Dwelling on past moments removes focus from being fully conscious in the present moment. Learn from them and move on with those lessons incorporated.

My Personal Paradigm

In my own operating paradigm, I run on several core suppositions. These have changed over the years, and I strongly suspect they shall change again with further research and experimentation. Among these is the tenet of didacticism, which states that we are here to learn. Specifically, I believe that the natural state of consciousness is unshackled from physical matter and does not know suffering. We are attached to these frail mortal forms, in my estimation, to understand what it is to be limited and, more importantly, to see what we do when we believe our comfort, security, or very existence is on the line. Do we choose to operate compassionately or selfishly? I believe we are meant to work toward compassion. We are here to learn grace and to gently help others learn as well. This is simply what I have come to believe through my meditations.

I share this part of my operating paradigm for the purpose of eliciting thought in you about what you believe the nature of this world is. It has been labeled a prison, a paradise, a proving ground, and so many other things. I believe it to be a classroom. I do not know whether one can pass or fail its course, but I do believe one can retake it many times. Whether out of assignment or self-enrollment, I cannot yet discern. You must decide for yourself what you believe the nature of this life may be, or if you even deem that question to be of importance. Of course, there are those who believe the entirety of existence to be contained in physical phenomena, but I feel magicians are, by nature, unlikely to ascribe to this viewpoint, as we become keenly aware of many facets of existence lurking just beyond physical measurement or outward detection. Although, to those who adhere to belief solely in base material substance, I would quote the famed physicist Max Planck, who stated: "I regard consciousness as fundamental. I regard matter as derivative from consciousness. We cannot get behind consciousness. Everything that we talk about, everything that we regard as existing, postulates consciousness."[7] Then again, of all scientists, I find physicists to be involved in the most similar pursuits to magicians. We are, in quite different ways, seeking answers to remarkably similar questions about the nature of being. Regardless, even a completely materialist viewpoint can be reconciled with your practice if you so prefer it.

It is important to think about views like this because a lot of your time is likely going to be preoccupied with questions. The greatest, deepest, and eldest of these questions is "why?" "Why?" is the question that is most thoroughly baked into us. It is the constant companion of toddlers and philosophers alike. So thoroughly and inextricably central to the human experience is this question that its pursuit has preoccupied us as far back as we have record of our musings, perhaps more than any other thing in our history. Philosophy, religion, science—all of these branches of thought seek to answer various whys. Why are we here? Why does the sun rise and set? Why do the tides come and go? Why do people behave cruelly to other people? Why do we experience linear time? Why do we die?

You began your journey with this book with your own why. You asked yourself why you were pursuing the art of magic. Has that answer changed since you last reflected on it? Why did you desire to undergo this transformation, with many steps and long hours of meditation and ritual, to achieve a new state of awareness? If you have dedicated yourself seriously to the exercises in this book, you will have undergone many hours of practice before reaching this page. This has been no small undertaking. If you have earnestly applied yourself to the exercises detailed in this book, and if I have not faltered in my explaining them, your life from here onward will be different. You are now able to perceive, with senses

---

7. Sullivan, *Observer*, 17.

previously muted, the flow of energy around you. You are tuned in to the silent communications of the eidolons as they reveal their seals. You wield tools previously unmanifested. All of this you have undertaken and achieved, and it is important to know why.

By now your practice has likely been established. The baseline techniques of magic in this system have been revealed to you. You have awoken to the flow of energy around and through you. You have achieved a state of abiding grace. You can communicate with eidolons, illuminate them, and call them. You have learned to do so in a circle of your own design, wielding a scepter of your will. You have created a sanctum in your psyche and allowed your hands to interface with the subtle flows around you. This is the totality of the foundation of your practice. You are a magician.

Now What?

The following pages of this chapter will endeavor to equip you with the resources to develop your own techniques, including developing your own emblems and rituals. In addition, this portion will seek to help you define your practice, set goals, introduce you to a small shorthand notation system for ritual work, and prompt you to establish nomenclature for talking about your practice. Following these subjects, we will discuss techniques for the advanced practitioner.

Emblems are tokens of a specific agreement between you, the magician, and an eidolon. There are many techniques for creating these emblems, but all revolve around the creation of an agreement. This is invariably done with an eidolon that you have previously established a steady working relationship with. One might enter their temple of mind, call an eidolon into a circle of their own design, and begin to converse. The practitioner and eidolon must then decide on a signal between them. This signal, referred to as an emblem, when given, will elicit a predetermined reaction from the eidolon who listens for it. An emblem can be a special word or phrase to utter, an item to wave in a certain pattern, a slip of paper with a specific symbol to rip or burn, or any such small and easily accomplished thing. In this way, an emblem can be thought of as a traditional "spell." As an example, you may be about to embark upon a frightening endeavor. You call an eidolon and ask that, in your time of need, they help you to master your fear. They agree, and you decide upon a word that, when you utter it, will speed them to your side to help dispel your fright. We will discuss further techniques and ideas for the creation of emblems in the following pages.

You are already familiar with rituals; they have played a large part in your arriving at this sentence. You have engaged in the Lesser Banishing Ritual of the Pentagram, as well as the Invocation of the Elementals. You have forged your scepter of art and made ready your scepter of artifice as its vessel. You have dedicated yourself to the work through the Circle of Concentric Ascension and sought beyond in the Passage of the Octa-decagon Gate. You understand how to perform rituals. To proceed further along your path, you should also be familiar with how to create them.

The creation of rituals is an art form that draws upon allegory and symbolism to influence the subconscious mind. It also conducts gathered energies in order to foster a specific state or achieve a desired outcome. In this section you will receive a toolbox with which you may build rituals to meet the goals and inquiries you pursue. These tools will include a set of shorthand symbols to aid in entering your rituals into your tome, as well as suggestions on linguistic and geometric choices, choreography where applicable, hand gestures, and optional ritual implements to incorporate. In addition, you will be given specific formulas for the creation of concise rituals designed to be enacted without the need for overly elaborate or time-consuming preparations or the procurement of obscure reagents.

Following instructions on ritual there will be an interlude before the next section in which you will be asked to reflect upon the goals of your practice and to define your practice further. In many ways, words are the vehicle of will, and through your words you may express the inner work-ings of your mind to other consciousnesses. Due to this, it is beneficial to understand the words you use to define your practice and what they mean to you.

Let us begin.

Forging Emblems

This system of magic is a contemplative one. It focuses on deep introspection and deep attunement to both oneself and one's surroundings. This is accomplished through meditation and ritual that emphasize forging connections with one's subconscious. In an internal paradigm, one can view eidolons as the inherent protocols of the psyche that function beyond surface level awareness. The issue that arises when interfacing in this manner is that there is little emphasis on alacrity. Effects are gleaned through meditation and ritual, and not every situation is suitable for these practices. Manifesting eidolons through use of their sigil and call is one way to circumvent the necessity for longer ritual once you have gained a level of comfort. Another more targeted solution is the use of emblems, which are meant to be used "out in the wild," or outside of a formal ritual space.

An emblem is a symbolic token, gesture, or action that an eidolon has agreed to respond to in a predetermined manner to aid you in a specified way. Whether you view this as a set signal to an external entity or a drumming up of a subconscious thoughtform, the result is the same. Remember that all things are interwoven, and your power stems chiefly from your will as a self-sovereign and compassionate consciousness acting upon the weaving that we physical beings mutually agree to call reality.

While a completed emblem is meant to be used while out and about, they are created in the temple of mind. To begin creating an emblem, you must first decide upon three essential components. Foremost you must decide on what you are hoping to achieve and why you are hoping to achieve it. Do you need help with a difficult mental task, such as quitting smoking or gaining the discipline to run a marathon or study for an exam? Do you need help establishing positive thought patterns? Do you wish for a tool to ward off ill intentions? These are all good candidates for emblem use. When you have decided on your purpose for your emblem, make an entry for the emblem in your tome. You can name your emblem by its purpose or think of any fanciful name that appeals to you. Once you know what your aim is, you need to ask yourself why you wish to accomplish it. Meditate on this goal and why it is important to you before proceeding on to the next step.

The second component is the actual nature of the emblem in the physical world. Is it a symbol like an eidolon's sigil that must be drawn? Is it a hand gesture, a word to utter, or even a whistle or hum? The essential consideration is that an emblem is not permanent. A permanent focal point for an eidolon or effect in this system is referred to as a gate, and the creation of gates is discussed in chapter 8. An emblem is akin to a spell. It is meant to trigger an instantaneous effect when evoked. For my emblems I most often use a word and hand gesture combination, but I have also made use of subtler means in situations where these would not be appropriate. A specific symbol drawn on paper works anywhere you may have a notebook. If you are having trouble deciding what to use, I recommend a hand gesture done with your hands charged as in the Blossoming Hand Meditation and paired with a word of your own creation.

Another consideration for the creation of emblems is the possibility of accidentally evoking them. It is best to choose specific things that one would not do randomly. When selecting words, it is better to fabricate one or use a word in another language than to use a word you may speak in conversation. Similarly, hand gestures of common use, such as a thumbs up or peace sign, make poor emblems. Anything you may absentmindedly say or do should be avoided.

Common emblem components may include but are not limited to:

- A word and gesture combination.
- The act of drawing a symbol.
- A specific set of motions made with a specific physical object, such as a wand.
- A specific sequence of notes, hums, or whistles.
- The act of tearing, burning, or submerging a specific small object or symbol.
- A rhyme or short phrase that would not arise in conversation.

Once you have named your emblem, decided upon its physical nature, and recorded this information in an entry in your tome, you are ready to decide on the last necessary component: which eidolon you wish to engage with to fulfill the emblem. It is important to reiterate that all power stems from the eternal and all-permeating energy of existence that inextricably flows through you as a conscious being. However, eidolons should be viewed as helping hands in a world where our own minds often trip us up. At this point, you should have a working relationship with several eidolons, a selection from this book and hopefully others you have illuminated yourself. You will, by now, have an idea of their personalities and what tasks they enjoy and excel at. This should give you an idea of which one to approach for the task at hand. Know which eidolon you plan to approach before proceeding, but do not record this in your tome until an agreement has been made.

It is possible the eidolon you select will not wish to engage in the work you are proposing, and that is fine. You should not press the matter if this is the case. Rather, thank them for their consideration and select another. It is also possible you may not have a single eidolon in your ark that wishes to collaborate on a specific emblem. This is rare but not unheard of. Generally, the broader use an emblem has, the easier it is to find an eidolon to work with on it, and the more niche, the more difficult it may be. For instance, almost any eidolon might be willing to help you create an emblem to ward off negative energies when you perceive them to be close. On the other hand, it may be slightly more difficult to find an eidolon interested in creating a specific emblem to help you master the art of origami. Eidolons have interests and talents too.

When you have selected the eidolon that you wish to approach, the next point is making an agreement. Eidolons, as a rule in my experience, do not ask you for things in return for their help. They do not exist in a state in which they need anything, and they are happy to assist if they are treated with respect and consideration, as we should give any colleague. If you find an eidolon asking you for things in return, I advise you dismiss them and do not seek further contact. I say this so that we understand that an agreement is not the same as a deal.

An agreement for an emblem or a gate, as we will discuss later, can be seen more as a script. You are eliciting an eidolon to be cast in the pageant of your magic, and they are deciding whether it interests them or not. If it does, you have an agreement, and your emblem is made. An emblem can be unmade any time in the same manner it was made. Simply contact the eidolon engaged in it, let them know it is no longer required, and you cordially dissolve the agreement. Etiquette goes a long way in dealing with eidolons.

To make an emblem, you will need the three components previously discussed: a desired effect, a trigger for that effect, and a candidate eidolon to aid in translating that effect into being. You will enact one of your centering exercises and enter your temple of mind. Once within, you will set your space with one of the appropriate rituals, understanding that your circle encompasses the entire mental temple. From there, you will call the eidolon that you have chosen and discuss the emblem you propose. In all likelihood, as this should be an eidolon you have experience working with, they will agree, and your emblem will be complete. The final step is to record which eidolon is facilitating the emblem in the emblem's entry in your tome.

To provide one very simple example, let us say that you have made an agreement with the first eidolon to help you overcome your hypothetical stage fright. You have decided that you will use a gesture and a phrase before going on stage. You will pass your open-palmed hand in front of your face and utter the phrase "all the world is a stage," and this will serve as an instantaneous signal to the first eidolon that you require the agreed upon assistance. Emblems are by design instantaneous effects. Sustained effect are accomplished in a similar but not identical manner using gates, which will be covered later.

A magician may have one or two go-to emblems or a collection of hundreds. You should review your emblems on occasion, meditating on them and cementing them in your mind. If you have many, it may also be a good idea to review them and see if they are still necessary. If they are not, simply dissolve them. Mark dissolved emblems as such in your tome, perhaps with a specific symbol. The ritual symbol for release serves this purpose well and is contained in the next section.

Creating Rituals

Where emblems serve as prepared shortcuts for your magic, rituals are the base unit by which the work is done when we have time and space to work at a measured pace. Your space-defining exercises are rituals, as is the Circle of Concentric Ascension, the Passage of the Octadecagon Gate, and the methods by which you brought your scepter of art into being. Calling eidolons involves a short form ritual. These rituals were introduced to you by a fellow magician in the sincere hope that you will adopt them and benefit from that adoption. We magicians share amongst ourselves so that our learning may become greater than the sum of its parts. Going forward, creating your own rituals, both for yourself and to share with others, will likely become an essential part of your magical toolbox.

Ritual work is predicated upon achieving an understanding of symbolism—the symbolism of colors, directions, images, objects, and narratives—which is used to produce allegorical formulas to manifest intentions. An entirely separate book could easily be dedicated to the penning of rituals by exhaustively elaborating upon the symbolic meanings of stones, plants, animals, gestures, and every other thing in the light of our sun and beyond. However, that is not the intention of this section, and there are already many books on such subjects. It is my intention to instruct you on a formula; a matrix into which you may plug your own icons of significance to draft rituals of meaning and substance to you.

All things that exist extrinsically exist intrinsically. This is to say that if an object exists in the world, it also must exist in the perception of consciousness. If there is a sword, there is the idea of a sword, which can be used to visualize a sword, and as such, all things may exist symbolically in ritual. Furthermore, many things are extant in the inner realm that do not currently exist in the outer realm, allowing for ritual symbols that have no physical world cognates. Suffice it to say, the well of symbolism for use in rituals in nearly inexhaustible, although most magicians seem to develop a certain set of symbolic components they will recycle throughout their work. This thematic palette will assist you in further defining your practice in the following section of this chapter.

It will be of use to you to develop a set of tools that serve to bring you into the ritual state of consciousness, which is a liminal state between waking reality and dreamlike trance in which you straddle the border of the physical and symbolic worlds. These tools should engage several senses at once. At the most basic level, and with no outside components, you can incorporate hand motions or total body choreography and the sound of your own humming or chanting. Expanding your component pouch, you can incorporate external objects to trigger sensory responses. I personally recommend incense or fragrant dried herbs. Scent has a powerful connection to memory, and building the association of a certain scent with ritual can be of use. Your new-world Abramelin oil can serve you here. You may also wish to incorporate special lighting, such as colored lanterns, or specific objects to visually mark the borders of your ritual space.

The essential ritual formula for this system is a six-step process as follows. Keep in mind, however, that you alone decide what works for you. It is your task to explore and determine what edits and variations of this ritual formula work for you, or to forge your own entirely new one if that is what you decide.

The Steps of a Ritual

1. Achieve a centered state.
2. Define your space.
3. Set your working intention.
4. Enact manifestation.
5. Release your effect.
6. Close your ritual.

The first step, achieve a centered state, is the precursor to all ritual work. In this step you will come to a place of calm, abiding, and present-moment awareness. This is usually done by engaging in a centering exercise such as the Middle Pillar, Rigpa Meditation, or White Thread Meditation. As you progress, you may become aware of other ways to bring yourself to this state, and those may serve here as well.

The second step, define your space, is the preamble to the intention work of the ritual. The Lesser Banishing Ritual of the Pentagram and the Invocation of the Elementals are ready-made exercises to define your space. By defining space, you are setting a boundary past which no magical effect not of your will may penetrate. You are also raising the energy within your space to a level that is powerfully charged with directionality of will. Defining space can be done in many ways and utilize many symbolic reagents, such as drawing a circle of salt, placing a crystal orb at each cardinal direction, or using an existing circle of standing stones, if you wish.

The third and fourth steps are those in which the largest share of the ritual work is done. In the third step, set your working intention, you will define the effect you wish to make manifest. By setting your working intention, you are stating aloud what you wish to achieve. Ritual language is often allegorical and poetic, and many practitioners find this adds to the beauty of the ritual and therefore enhances their experience; however, this is not a requirement. The efficacy of a ritual is determined by will, not linguistic aptitude.

In the fourth step, enact manifestation, you will define and carry out how you are to bring your previously stated intention into being. This is where you might call upon eidolons, direct energies, and beseech the subroutines of existence through allegorical instruction. You will be gathering energies, solidifying them, and feeling them coalesce around you. This step will likely cause you to feel a charge in the air or a static vibration that defies the physical sense's ability to categorize. You will gather your will around you and feel it weave itself into being.

In the fifth step, release your effect, you will conduct the energy of manifestation you have gathered and spur it forth, allowing it to expand as of its own will and strain at the boundaries of your circle, yearning to make itself real. This can be done through verbal command, physical gesture, or the use of physical materials, such as incense, herbs, or ritual tools.

Finally, step six, close the circle, is the shortest step. It involves formally thanking any entities you have worked with or asked to watch over you, dissolving your circle, and stepping out of the ritual mindset and back into everyday operation.

To illustrate these six steps, I will give you a sample ritual communicated step-by-step to provide further clarity. This ritual has the simple intention of releasing healing into the world to do spontaneous and self-propagating good, seeding compassion wherever it can. You need not actually perform this ritual; simply read it that it may serve as an example of the steps just described.

Sample Ritual

Step 1: Perform the Rigpa Meditation. This should be done until a calm, centered state is achieved.

Step 2: Place a stone orb or obelisk at every cardinal direction, equidistant from the center where you stand. Using a pouch of salt and dried rosemary, call the quarters and sprinkle the rosemary salt each time you turn. (This is part of this particular ritual design, but physical implements are never strictly necessary, so do not feel your designs must incorporate them. I have chosen salt and rosemary in this instance for their symbolic representations of purity and love, respectively.)

Step 3: Face the east and set your intention. Hold your scepter above your head and hold your nondominant hand down at your side, open palmed with fingers facing the ground and palm facing forward, stating:

"Archangels, guides, benevolence within and around me, I ask that you gather here and watch over my work. I stand in a circle of my will and hold above my head the scepter of my art, attend me. Abide with me as I enact this work with the intention of bringing healing into this world to go forth, amplify compassion wherever it abides, and kindle it where it does not."

Step 4: Bring your hands in front of you. Place the top of your scepter roughly at eye level. Place your empty hand, with fingers slightly curled as if holding an invisible orb, positioned about a foot away horizontally from the top of the scepter. Keep your elbows slightly bent. Your arms should be relaxed enough to hold the position for a few minutes. Begin to draw energy through the central conduit established in your meditation and coalesce it, envisioning it traveling through your dominant hand, up your scepter, and gathering at the top in a glowing sphere. Through your nondominant hand, envision the energy arcing from your palm, down your fingertips, and into the orb forming at the top of your scepter. As you engage in this, say the following:

"I call you to witness, ineffable geometers of the Most High. You beneficent spirits whom the children of mortality have named angels, devas, amesha spentas, bodhisattvas, ascended magicians, and numberless epithets lost to the ages. Beings of powerful joy whose faces are facets in the jewels of myriad faiths, attend me. Anoint me with the chrisms of compassion and lend me your radiant power. I draw forth this power to banish evil. I draw forth this power to amplify compassion. I draw forth this power to heal the unseen wounds of this world. I charge this power with a thirsting justice, an unrelenting kindness, and my own inexorable will."

Continue to draw forth energy until the air around you has been altered by the static of its presence and you feel its fullness like a sun in your hands. This step is usually where one would call eidolons by name to aid in the work, if desired.

Step 5: When you have achieved what you believe to be critical mass, speak the following words purposefully:

"Having gathered thus, I charge you go forth and make thyself manifest. Go forth! Illuminate each crevice of existence and flush out hatred. Go forth! Heal the invisible wounds inflicted by the errant malice of the likewise wounded. Go forth, and with each passing moment, grow ever brighter with the good you will do! I send you hence! Do this for the collective good and with harm to none. When this circle is dismissed, go forth!"

Now swing your scepter and empty hand outward, making an arc in front of you until you are standing in a T-pose. As you do so, feel the orb of energy you have coalesced expand, straining against the sphere of your sanctum from within.

Step 6: Remain in a T-pose and say:

"When my arms fall, this circle is no more, and all energies within may speed forth to their intention. My thanks to all agents of the Most High here in attendance. Go in peace and watch over all who enact the great work. As I have spoken, so I have created."

Let your arms fall to your sides and visualize your circle dissolving, releasing all gathered energy outward in all directions. Take a single deep, slow breath and place your scepter on the ground or any altar you may have within your space. Speak a capstone utterance. In this case, say:

"So it is."

Your ritual has ended.

The rituals you develop will serve you well if recorded in detail. Unlike an eidolon's information, the rituals you design should be shared freely with those in need of them as long as they do not include the names of eidolons. Rituals can call upon eidolons in steps 3 and/or 4, or you can eschew that entirely and work solely from your will. It is beneficial to think of eidolons as existential or subconscious helper protocols that can be utilized to aid you, and while that aid is excellent, it is not strictly necessary. Since a ritual can have any eidolon "plugged in," so to speak, they are eidolon agnostic, and any magician can use them by altering the language to invoke the eidolon or eidolons of their choice or no eidolon at all.

The ritual example provided uses physical reagents and elaborate language. These are matters of preference, as it aids many in achieving a state of ritual consciousness. I cannot reiterate enough that these are embellishments rather than necessities.

Rituals often deal with things like the directionality of energy; the representation of elements; the ideas of other realms of existence, such as planes or dimensions; and metaphorical states of matter and energy. To aid you in recording these rituals in your tome, notation symbols can be of great benefit. Notation symbols are just shorthand to represent common ritual drafting concepts. Following is a selection of such symbols to aid you in your work:

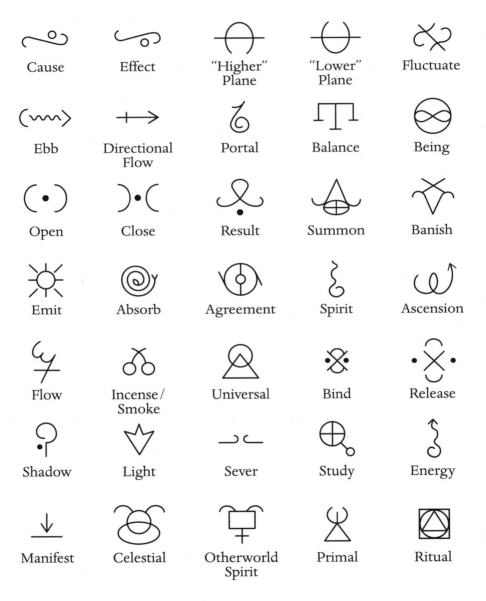

Cause	Effect	"Higher" Plane	"Lower" Plane	Fluctuate
Ebb	Directional Flow	Portal	Balance	Being
Open	Close	Result	Summon	Banish
Emit	Absorb	Agreement	Spirit	Ascension
Flow	Incense / Smoke	Universal	Bind	Release
Shadow	Light	Sever	Study	Energy
Manifest	Celestial	Otherworld Spirit	Primal	Ritual

Ritual Notation Symbols

Defining Your Practice

Over the course of this book, you have encountered several terms for practitioners of the great work that is magic. We have used the catchall term *magician*, as well as the term *adept*, which is defined as any who have come through this system of magic past the Circle of Concentric Ascension and begun to work with eidolons. However, you are encouraged to develop your own nomenclature for your practice. This includes terms you use to refer to yourself, your tools, and any working group you may form. At this point, you have developed your own personalized touches and interpretations, and you may have begun to see patterns in the emblems and rituals you create. Identifying these stylistic tendencies will help you to develop a lexicon for your practice.

Language is arbitrary; unlike mathematics, it is not universal. While an item of a certain volume will displace the same amount of water under any name, the name of an item changes depending upon language, dialect, regionalism, slang, and other factors. Language is not a measurement of existence like shape and weight. It is a way to communicate concepts between conscious beings who share that language. I make this distinction to encourage you to not get hung up on terminology. For instance, some magicians will argue over whether the art should be spelled *magic* or *magick*. The idea here is that using a *k* at the end differentiates the art from parlor tricks plied by illusionists. I do not ascribe to this conceit because, to my understanding, the word *magic* comes from the Greek *magos*, which is derived from the old Persian *magus*, which described the Persian priestly class, such as the three magi of biblical fame. The root of this word means something akin to "to possess power."[8] This means the origin of the word *magic* was meant to describe exactly what we are engaged in here, and only in later ages did it begin to take on the meaning of stage illusion. Therefore, I spell *magic* as it comes down to us from the ancients, unadulterated by the linguistic expectations of Victorian society. However, I also acknowledge that this question of spelling barely matters—if it matters at all. When

---

8. Online Etymology Dictionary, "Magic," accessed August 2, 2022, https://www
.etymonline.com/word/magic.

we speak of magic/k among one another, we magicians all know we are speaking of the same thing, and that is what matters.

Similarly, the way you define your practice exists chiefly to assist you and those you may work with in navigating the concepts central to your practice. Whether you wish to call yourself a witch, sorcerer, warlock, priest, priestess, mage, wizard, conjurer or any such thing is entirely your business and no one else's as long as it does not co-opt the honorifics of an existing cultural tradition into which you have not been initiated. However, it is important that you have a definition for this term that aids you in explaining it to those you may wish to collaborate with. For my part, I generally refer to myself as a magician, sorcerer, or invoker. You may develop a working group, and that group may have its own terminology. You may agree among yourselves to call the group a circle and have all members collectively be referred to as celebrants. You could also call your group a book club and its members readers. There is truly no correct or incorrect terminology.

You should explore your practice as you progress, and this will aid you in defining core concepts. For example, you may decide that you only wish to work with a specific subset of otherworld spirits that you understand to have strong ties with nature, whether defined by you as external intelligences or internal primordial facets of your own mind. You may decide that, in order for you to feel purposeful in your rituals, all your rituals must incorporate plant matter, such as herbs, branches, or flowers. You may decide that all your eidolon calls must involve a statement of thanks to the earth. These are ways of defining your practice and tailoring it to you. Explore what feels correct for you as you work, and make note of it in your tome.

Using Mantras

Continuing with the subject of language, let us discuss mantras. In the traditional Vedic sense, a mantra is a word or phrase used to aid in meditation. In a more general parlance, it is a slogan one might repeat to emphasize a view of the world or strongly held belief, often an aphorism. The way we will use mantras here falls somewhere between these two notions. We will use mantras to quickly establish a centered state of calm abiding.

There are many wonderful mantras already extant that one can draw from, but I encourage you to develop your own. This should be a simple statement that reminds you to be present and aware, witnessing the current moment without grasping for anything you wish to possess or fearing anything you wish to avoid. I often use the mantra "I am an infinite being experiencing what it is to be limited." This reminds me that whatever tribulations I may experience are fleeting facets of this world and can only assail my inner peace insofar as I allow them to.

Use your tome to reflect on what statements remind you of your own nature as a perceiving consciousness beyond body or mind. When you have selected one to try, meditate using one of the centering exercises you encountered in chapter 2. When you have finished the centering portion and are abiding in a calm state, repeat the mantra you have chosen aloud and note how it feels. If it works for you, it should feel like a peaceful ripple in your consciousness. It should not feel like an escalation or de-escalation of your sustained calm but instead a stirring within it—a resonance. If it does not feel correct to you, try a different mantra next time.

When you have settled on the first mantra you wish to use, record it in your tome. You can have as many more as you find helpful, but you should have at least one mantra of affirmation. You can repeat this mantra when you achieve a state of calm, abiding in meditation with the goal to associate the mantra with this state so that when you utter it out in the world or simply think it while taking a deep breath, it can bring you to a state of present-moment awareness. The mantra should become your shortcut to a meditative state when you feel yourself slipping. The goal, of course, is to always abide in this state, but it can be a difficult one to achieve amid the din of modern life.

Repeating your mantra while in a short meditation is a beneficial exercise, and it may be helpful for you to use some form of recitation beads as a physical aid. These beads are ubiquitous to human efforts to count verses, usually prayers. Some examples from around the world are mala beads, rosary beads, and *misbaha*. I would recommend you produce a set of recitation beads for your efforts. You will use them by holding the beads in one hand and sliding them one by one through your thumb and forefinger, keeping track of your mantra repetitions.

As always, I recommend you make your own tools or purchase them from an artisan rather than seek a mass-produced object simply due to the respect with which it will have already been treated. I make my own strands of 108 beads with a knot between each bead. Incredibly beautiful bead strands can be made very cheaply out of wood, glass, or semiprecious stone beads. Experiment with colors and patterns that you find meaning in. I find 8-millimeter beads to be the ideal size for me, but you may prefer beads of a different size depending on how they feel in your hands.

Creating Your Own Meditation Beads

To create your own beads, you will need:

- approximately six feet of woven nylon or silk cord 0.8 millimeters in diameter
- 99 or 108 8-millimeter stone or wooden beads with holes large enough to fit your cord, ideally 1 millimeter

You will need to string these beads together, usually with a small knot between each bead, and then tie the two ends of your resulting strand together. There is a diagram to assist you in this endeavor.

The color combination of these beads is your choice. I have made many sets of beads over the years, and my favorite set is of simple white agate. You may wish to intersperse beads that match the colors of the chakras or Sephiroth down one side of your set of beads. This is both symbolically indicative of their purpose and aesthetically pleasing.

If you wish to add chakra representations, you should keep all other beads a uniform neutral color. As you make your strand, place a red bead as your third bead, and replace every third bead with a bead matching the next ascending chakra color until all seven are placed. This should result in a loop that, on the one side, contains each chakra color in ascending of order red, orange, yellow, green, blue, indigo, and violet.

To instead add representations of the Sephiroth, use a neutral color that is not black or white for all other beads. As you make your strand, place a black bead as your fourth bead, and replace every fourth bead with a bead matching the next ascending Sephira color until all five are placed. This should result in a loop that, on one side, contains each Sephira color in ascending order of black, purple, gold or yellow, silver or gray, and white.

Your strand can be worn as a necklace when not in use. When worn in this way, the chakra or Sephiroth pattern should be on the side of your dominant hand. Alternatively, the strand can be wrapped around the wrist of your dominant hand and worn as a bracelet.

These recitation beads, like all physical tools, are optional enhancements to your practice.

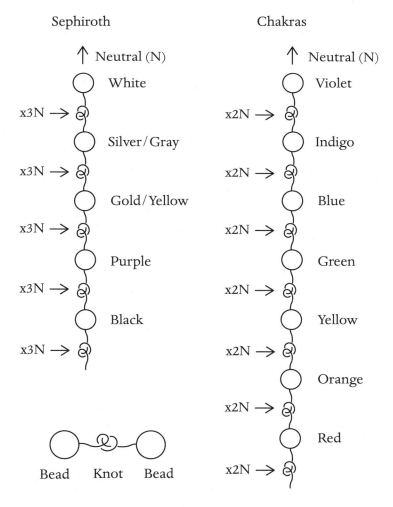

Sephiroth   Chakras

↑ Neutral (N)   ↑ Neutral (N)

White   Violet

x3N →   x2N →

Silver/Gray   Indigo

x3N →   x2N →

Gold/Yellow   Blue

x3N →   x2N →

Purple   Green

x3N →   x2N →

Black   Yellow

x3N →   x2N →

Orange

x2N →

Bead   Knot   Bead   Red

x2N →

Bead Layout

In this chapter, you have learned to observe yourself and your magical practice as you grow together. You have built steadily upon the foundations of your craft, learning to adapt and develop your own rituals, forge emblems, define your practice, and develop tools to aid you in the daily maintenance of your centered awareness. Ahead, you will expand upon this knowledge and learn more advanced ways to interact with eidolons, create sustained effects through gates, and become aware of still more entities inhabiting your invisible or allegorical world.

Chapter 8
TECHNIQUES FOR THE ADVANCED PRACTITIONER

———————◦———————

The following techniques are meant to expand your thaumaturgical repertoire through the introduction of new ways to work with the host of your own ark, which is the section of your tome used to chronicle the details of the eidolons you have met. At this point in your journey, you should have developed your own emblems, rituals, and entirely new arts tailored to your unique practice. The exercises to follow represent further ways to deepen your engagement with magic and explore the concepts previously put forth. These techniques are optional explorations and have been grouped together under the advanced category as they represent entirely new concepts that have the potential to refocus your work down new avenues.

Several of the techniques we are about to explore are not to be approached lightly. They begin to blur the lines between the inner and outer world and should not be attempted without first achieving a sustained state of centered awareness. As you are aware, magic involves tapping into the raw energy of existence. The deeper you wade into the river of the arcane, the more powerful the currents become, and you must remain centered in yourself to avoid being swept away. The exercises to follow represent the outskirts of readily quantifiable practice. Past them lies a fathomless depth of ever-expanding awareness that can indelibly and inexorably change the way you perceive yourself and the notion of existence.

Establishing a Convocation

A convocation is a working group of eidolons that serve as counsel to the magician to help them cultivate behaviors or practices. The recommended first convocation consists of three eidolons, though you may wish to establish more than one convocation of three. The grouping of these eidolons is entirely up to the needs of your practice, but I have found that a convocation comprised of one otherworld spirit, one celestial, and one primal works well in most general applications. The three eidolons called in your Passage of the Octadecagon Gate are a natural choice for your first convocation. Alternatively, once you have a matured ark, three convocations of three eidolons with specific commonalities can form an especially useful council. The convocations I most often invoke always contain at least one celestial as a reminder to be working toward goals of an aspirational nature.

Establishing convocations allows the eidolons involved to weave themselves in and out of your daily life. Due to this, it is advisable that you draw upon eidolons representing and embodying the highest positive qualities of aspiration to establish a convocation. When you establish a convocation, keep in mind which eidolon's words you would most welcome interjecting in your day and suggesting courses of action.

Establishing a convocation is much like asking an eidolon to serve as a guide; however, it comes with some more nuance. You are no longer asking simply for assistance yourself but for eidolons to work together and harmonize their energies for your benefit. To do this, you will enter your temple of mind and call each eidolon you wish to invite into the convocation. I find it best to visualize a specific chamber for this purpose—a meeting room or council chamber with seats for each eidolon can serve here. Personally, I often envision a circle of solid gemstone thrones suspended in the vastness of space or an amphitheater in a temple that floats upon an island in the sky.

In this chamber, you will discuss what you wish to cultivate and develop. This can range from qualities such as patience, generosity, discipline, or self-love to tangible skills such as mastering a musical instrument or learning a language. Discuss with each eidolon how they can help and set boundaries as to where or when you would like them to avoid giving counsel. Once all are agreed but before you leave your temple of mind and part ways with your convocation, you will design a seal that will serve to call your convocation. From now on, when you wish to hold a formal meditative meeting of your convocation, you need only call them using this seal rather than calling each eidolon individually.

Convocations do not need to be established for a specific purpose, but they can also be used as shortcuts to work with a group of eidolons you have an affinity for. If you find you are often working with more than one eidolon, forming a convocation removes the need to call them all individually. These convocations are simply formed for general counsel and collaboration.

Aside from a seal, you may wish to assign your convocation a name to aid in calling it. This is not strictly necessary, but it can be useful if you have more than one convocation. When you establish a convocation, you should make note of its seal, name if present, goal if applicable, and members in your tome.

Calling convocations is somewhat simpler than calling individual eidolons, as the legwork has been done ahead of time. All convocation members have previously agreed to work together, and they are already listening carefully for opportunities to lend their advice. As such, you may simply focus on their seal while in your temple of mind and make a small formal announcement along the lines of: "Convocation whose seal is before me, attend this chamber that we may meet in good faith and fellowship." If you have named the convocation, refer to it by name. For example: "Violet Sun Convocation, whose seal is before me, attend this chamber that we may meet in good faith and fellowship."

Establishing convocations is also a preparatory step for highly advanced work that lies beyond the octadecagon gate and in the realms of the outer host. Specifically, one can function as a nexus, forming a convocation between all eidolons of their host and allowing them to harmonize and pass freely into and out of manifestation. This requires a bedrock of trust and several years of working with the eidolons of your ark. It is a technique that may be discussed in a future work.

After learning to call up convocations, thus enabling more than one eidolon to maintain continuous communication, we will move on to the creation of gates. Gates often employ an eidolon or eidolons to watch over them in much the same way the eighteenth eidolon watches over the octadecagon gate.

Creating Gates

Gates are permanent or semipermanent loci of will where effects are woven into being. While an emblem is a single instantaneous trigger of a predetermined effect, gates are persistent and lasting epicenters of effect. This can mean that they are always active or that they lay dormant and activate on certain conditions. Most eidolons are capable of making informed decisions as to when a predetermined condition has truly been satisfied. Previously, we equated emblems to spells. Here, we may likewise equate gates with amulets, talismans, or any other various enchantments of items and locations.

A gate programs your will upon reality through the use of a self-sustaining focal point of energy. This is an energy pattern you will create and charge in much the same way you did with your scepters. This energy pattern will be represented in your tome by its own seal, which should hint at, through your own artistic sensibilities, the flow of that energy pattern as well as its purpose. These two tasks, manifesting your energy pattern and documenting the design and purpose of the gate, are the foundational steps of gate creation.

When establishing a gate, you should enter a focused and aware state, feeling the flow of energy through the central column you are now familiar with. Focus on the energy flowing through you and extend your dominant hand, your scepter of art manifesting therein. As you feel the purpose of your gate resonate in you, envision lines of light extending from your scepter and weaving the pattern of the gate into being in the air before you. Perhaps you are making a gate that you will place on a protective charm or use to ward off negative wills from a home. Let the gate take the shape of its purpose.

When your gate is made and documented in your tome, the next step is to apply that gate to some sort of object or space. There are two ways to accomplish this. The first is to simply visualize and overlay the gate into the desired target and then envision it manifesting its own small pillar of light through its center, essentially directing it to plug in to the ambient energy of existence and thus sustain its effect independently. The second way is to call an eidolon and ask them to steward the gate and cause it to activate or change its effects based upon criteria you put forth or simply to renew its potency if it begins to fade. An eidolon can keep their attention on a vastly greater number of simultaneous tasks than a physically incarnated being.

Gates vary in duration and strength based upon the conviction placed in their making and the complexity of their purpose. The more difficult a gate's task, the more likely it will need to be renewed periodically. Likewise, the more casually the gate was made, the more likely it will need renewing in short order. One should not go about creating gates if their heart is not in it; those gates will prove ephemeral at best.

While using physical representations of the gate patterns themselves is not strictly necessary, it can be beneficial and aesthetically pleasing to depict them on the item or area of effect. This can manifest as simply as drawing the gate pattern on a piece of paper and pinning it to a wall or as intricately as etching it into a pendant or carving it in stone. Gates can also make for potent protective or empowering tattoos.

Gates have to do with the energetic conditions of a specific anchor in space, whether a place or a physical object, and they are not unbound from physicality and able to transverse space-time unimpeded as some other entities may be. They can often attract or repel protoconscious entities known as vestiges, which we will discuss in the upcoming section on tonal resonance.

Tonal Resonance

The practice of tonal resonance is perhaps the only exercise in this book that may strictly require the use of a physical tool. This can only be avoided if you have perfect pitch and can sing or whistle an absolutely accurate scale of some sort. Tonal resonance is a technique that runs on the principle that internal and external forces respond to vibrations. In this case, these are vibrations that manifest as audible sound.

To elaborate on the usefulness of this technique, it is necessary to discuss a new concept. Namely, the idea of vestiges. Vestiges are not eidolons. While an eidolon is a self-manifesting intelligence, either an external unembodied consciousness or an internal subconscious facet depending on your paradigm, a vestige is a rudimentary string of emotion or inspiration that does not manifest in a way that can be communicated with linguistically or symbolically. Vestiges are energy patterns that communicate with waves of emotion, bursts of intuition, or snippets of melody and patterned sound or light. Unlike an eidolon, with which you may have coherent, even linguistic communication, vestiges simply emit their chosen signal repetitively unless they receive tonal input that may cause them to alter it. I envision vestiges very similarly to jellyfish floating about a vast sea of energy. Depending on your paradigm, you may see them as internalized patterns and ingrained habits or as literal energetic protoconscious thoughtforms.

Tonal resonance uses clear notes to influence the movements of vestiges. Vestiges can come to linger in places, both in the world and in the psyche, and they should be encouraged to continue along on their way. If not, they will create patterns that those who are not abiding in a centered state can become ensnared in. Vestiges often cling to places where specific behavioral patterns or emotions were repeated over long periods of time.

Tools for tonal resonance are many, and any portable instrument can suffice. If you are not already musically inclined, I personally recommend a kalimba for its ease of use and portability. More elaborate alternatives are sets of bells, tuning forks, or singing bowls. Any portable implement that can produce consistent, clear notes in a discernible scale is suitable. If you are—or wish to become—musically proficient, I find that traditional woodwinds are uniquely suited to this technique. The ability to capture subtle tonal changes through breath enhances this modality greatly. The *xiao, quena, shakuhachi, bansuri,* Anasazi flute, and many other similar wooden or bamboo flutes make excellent companions to this technique. These flutes, if appropriately sized and sufficiently sturdy, can also double as utilitarian scepters of artifice.

Tonal resonance can be used to both detect and shepherd vestiges. To begin, one should enter a meditative state while holding their chosen resonant implement. It is then required that one listen with the heart, so to speak. It may be necessary to sound a few probing notes. The goal is to feel patterns of emotion or habit lingering in the air or in the mind and, once they're found, to sound a note that feels as if it corresponds to that pattern in a harmonious manner. This should elicit a change, which should then inspire another note. This is a languid dance of sorts—a slow call and response—and the longer it goes, the calmer and more fluid feeling the presence of the vestige should become. Eventually, it will dislodge itself and begin to drift along the currents of energy again, disentangled. At this point, you may leave it to float along on its own again or attempt to direct it in a simple way.

Vestiges are not capable of language; they are primordial and rudimentary forms of consciousness. Much in the way a mushroom or mollusk exists in a state that defies tidy classification as plant or animal, so does a vestige exist at a hazy junction before energy is defined as conscious or nonconscious. You can attempt to convey simple requests, such as to stay nearby or leave this area, but it is more akin to emitting an attractant or repellent signal than to making a verbal request.

To assign intentionality to a vestige would be remiss. They do not make decisions. They exist in a state of alien awareness from which they can respond to sonic and/or energetic stimuli. As such, it would be irresponsible to refer to them as possessing such developed manifestations of will as intentional malevolence or benevolence. They have effects on the areas they inhabit and the people who inhabit those areas along with them. Poisonous fumes are harmful, but we cannot call them intelligently evil. Penicillin is beneficial, but we cannot assign it a will to do good. Similarly, vestiges can have harmful or helpful effects on the areas in which they linger, but we cannot assign them such complex moral philosophies as good or evil. Remember this when interacting with them.

Tonal resonance can also be used to interact with natural loci of energy and other lingering energy forms that can be stirred to attention with harmonic sequences. Certain gates can be activated by melodies, and you can design your own gates to respond to musical notes or patterns if you wish. Tonal resonance is a highly nuanced and artistic practice, but it proves an incredibly useful one for communicating with energetic patterns and entities that may not understand linguistic forms of communication.

Along the same conceptual avenues inhabited by vestiges lie the concept of energetic blockages, or places where the flow of energy, the infinite patterns of the invisible world, become tangle and stagnant. These blockages are nonconscious areas of heaviness. They are places where ill intent was wrought or tragedy occurred. Often, they will attract baleful vestiges like beacons.

When encountering a blockage, it is necessary to attempt to dissolve it. These stagnant areas are unhealthy for the flow of energy and for the beings who encounter them. Oftentimes, the work of dissolving blockages necessitates first dislodging the vestiges attracted to them. One can do this in the way described above. The blockage itself can be seen like a complex knot or puzzle box. You must tease out its patterns with your will and direct energy until it crumbles with a great energetic sigh. This can often take multiple attempts with the aid of several eidolons or fellow magicians, but it is meaningful work that clears space for new wonders to manifest.

Listening Meditation

One way to attune yourself to the presence or passage of vestiges and the proximity of blockages is to learn to listen deeply. You are already cultivating these skills through your work with the eidolons, but in the following section, you will be presented with a meditation designed to hone your skills of esoteric listening, not with the ears but with senses beyond them.

The listening meditation, which I also call the unmanifested meditation, is a meditation I theorize would be best practiced in a sensory deprivation chamber. Unfortunately, few of us have ready access to such a thing, so we must make do with what we have. For my part, I use a pair of earplugs, a light-blocking sleep mask, and a reclining chair. If you engage in this meditation, be sure that you are in a safe place and can still hear emergency notifications, such as your fire alarm. I recommend that you do not leave candles or incense burning or anything in the oven.

The idea behind this meditation is that when the senses of the physical body are dampened or ignored, other more subtle senses can be employed. I came to this meditation because I have always been able to see certain patterns of energy that I cannot fully explain. Over the years of my childhood, I spent many long hours observing these patterns and how they reacted or failed to react to various stimuli. I concluded that it was not my eyes seeing these patterns but some other sense to which my visual perception of the things around me offered competing input.

Over the years, I have learned to navigate the world with this overlay to my vision, and I often find it barely noticeable during my daily tasks unless I focus on it deliberately. I posit I am seeing some sort of energy, but it could also be an unidentified medical anomaly; I do not profess to have all the answers. I have far too many questions for that to be the case. You will find that the more strange and incredible things you see, the less you presume to know and the more questions you will have.

Similarly, in deep meditation I have at times heard a ringing or chiming sound. The origin is unknown to me but the sound is pleasant and calming. These experiences inspired me to develop this sensory deprivation meditation to simply listen to existence and view the energy around me. This meditation exists to bring you to a place of complete receptivity, and I count it as an advanced technique because it involves utterly emptying the vessel of your mind.

This meditation is as simple as finding a dark place to assume a comfortable position to relax your body and clear your mind. You will wear a blindfold and earplugs and begin by breathing deeply and exhaling slowly as you focus on each muscle group in your body and relax each one. Then, you will begin to eschew your thoughts. Do not force this. The more one forces emptiness, the more filled it usually becomes with frustration.

Simply watch each errant thought as it drifts into your mind and watch it pass. Do not hold on to it but also do not scorn it. Just let it float away in its own time. Continue this until there are no more thoughts on the horizon. At this point, listen, breathe steadily, and wait.

I cannot tell you what you will see or hear in this meditation because it will be unique each time. Sometimes it will provide you only with relaxation, and sometimes it will provide you with visions, stories, sounds, and emotions. I can only guarantee that it will take practice to achieve a state of empty receptivity. You should make note of all that occurs in your working book each time you engage in this exercise.

To prepare you for the manner of visions you may receive, I can share an anecdote from one of my own working books. This experience occurred on an evening in July of 2020. I had just finished engraving a brass tag to be used as an anchor for a protective gate to be given to a close friend and decided to cap the evening off with a listening meditation. I spent a few minutes clearing my mind of errant thought before I began to experience a pleasant sensation of calm attunement to the quiescence. In short order, I found myself sitting on a lotus cushion carved of brilliant, luminous quartz set in the middle of a vast slow-moving river of great beauty.

Behind me, attached to my lotus seat at its base, ran a thin walkway of silver-gray stone. I often see structures made of this material in my meditative visions. The walkway led to a distant shore from which an elaborate temple complex rose against a mountainous backdrop of watercolor hues. As I sat in meditation in the physical realm, so, too, did I sit in meditation on this crystal lotus in my vision. During this meditation, any errant thoughts became blossoms that sprang from my brow, drifted onto the waters, and were carried away.

As time passed, a snake came toward me on the surface of the water. It motioned as if to strike but then, seeing I was unafraid of it, curled up beside me on my seat instead. Soon, I saw fish in the water gathering around, salmon and carp, and a long-necked turtle of nephrite green that approached and rested its head upon the base of the lotus. Not long afterward, a white crane waded through the river and stopped next to me, resting its head upon my left knee and raising one leg, opposite the snake that slept on my right. Several minutes passed in this way until I began to hear sweet music drifting over the surface of the water. This seemed to be a signal of sorts that caused the vision to shimmer and recede, signaling an end to my meditation for the evening.

I share this experience to give you an idea of the sort of things you might see, wonderful and strange, so that you will not be alarmed if you find yourself in a similar state of intense meditative visualization. Familiarity with this kind of vivid visualization will help you to prepare yourself for the following advanced technique, channeling eidolons.

Channeling Eidolons

I have one more advanced technique to impart to you in this chapter. Indeed, this next technique is the final practice I will impart in this book, and I hesitated to include this section at all. It is the absolute edge of this form of practice. After it, the boundaries melt away and the edges of magic blur into the experimental journey of consciousness that is truly advanced work.

In this section, I will discuss channeling eidolons. This is the practice of manifesting eidolons through your own body and allowing them to speak directly through you. It is something I do not advise you do until you have had several years working with the eidolon you wish to channel and, even then, only if you have established a bedrock of self-sovereign and centered awareness.

I caution you against taking this practice lightly. This is not due to any malice on the part of the eidolons (I do not believe they are capable of such) but rather that the eidolons represent powerful forces of subconscious significance. To conjure up that power—from wherever it may reside—and don its mantle for a time is by itself no small matter. However, greater still is the task of taking that mantle off. Without a truly unassailable center, one could easily become lost in the current of a deeply primordial thoughtform.

I began the practice of channeling earlier than I should have, as I was involved in this work from a young age, having carried it over from previous incarnations. Only by drawing upon experiences from before this life—and by sheer providence—did I not lose myself in the depth of the primordial root-consciousnesses that I have touched. Having now been engaged in this practice for some time, I can achieve the conduit state very easily and with little fanfare. It is possible for me to manifest an eidolon to deliver a message or short conversation channeled for a friend and then just as easily let them dissolve into background consciousness. I do not do this often, and it is not something I would advise to anyone who has not spent decades engaged in the practices detailed in this book.

However, channeling eidolons can be immensely beneficial as a tool to help others and, eventually, for self-help as well. When you first begin channeling an eidolon, it will be like riding a wave. It is by your will that you will catch the wave, and it will be your choice when to bail, but the duration in between those points will be you hanging on for the ride, and the twists and turns will be something of a blur. While you will be present during the conversation, you will not remember much of what was said afterward.

Eventually, you will begin to master the art and learn to navigate each whirlpool and eddy. It is at that point that you will be able to be present alongside the eidolon for every conversational nuance if you wish to be and to recall them in the process. However, when you are channeling for another, it is still sometimes best to hang back and give whomever you are channeling for some privacy.

This is the most difficult practice for me to communicate to you because it is the one that is the most nuanced and subtle to perform. It is not a ritual so much as the act of creating a doorway in your mind that is shaped to receive a specific eidolon. Further, when the eidolon approaches through that door, it is as a raw swell of consciousness, as if a dam had burst in the distance, and your task is to not only withstand the flood but to direct it to condense and fill a single chair from which it may converse for a time.

I cannot provide you with a step-by-step guide here. Channeling is not something everyone has the knack for, and those who do come into the talent differently. I can say that it will start by forging a strong bond with an eidolon, receiving them as a guide, and working with them often. Once you have this relationship in place, you can discuss with them whether they would be open to working through you in this capacity. They will guide you from there.

It is impossible to list detailed instruction on a technique that, by definition, should be unique to the nuances of your mind. However, it is my duty to inform you on how to set yourself right if your initial forays into channeling go awry. Luckily, in order to channel an eidolon, it is necessary for you to have developed a close bond with them. In this way, any eidolon you channel will have your best interests at heart. Still, out of an abundance of caution, you should only channel in a circle and in a tranquil state. Once again, I stress that you should have several years of working with an eidolon successfully before attempting channeling, and I must absolve myself of all responsibility for any difficulties you may encounter if you ignore this counsel. Indeed, as we are all unique, I can take no responsibility for your channeling at all. Only you can judge if it is something you are ready and able to do. Do not take it lightly.

If you do attempt a channeling and find it to be too much for you, know that you can move through it unscathed. An eidolon cannot stay channeled of their own volition. They are there at your permission and will leave the second that permission is revoked. They, by and large, only wish to communicate clearly. However, if you have channeled them and not been at a ready state, the sheer experience can be overwhelming and leave you unsettled after their departure, which often manifests as waves of sensory information or vision-like thought-streams. In order to pull yourself from this state, you will need to practice your preferred centering exercise followed by several hours of either sleep, meditation, or a low-stress activity, such as walking, reading, or practicing an art or craft.

Conclusion

PURSUING THE
TOTAL GOAL

B efore we conclude our time together, I must depart from the endeavor of offering techniques for your perusal and personalization and embark instead down a more ontological avenue. At this point in your practice, if you have been reading and following along with the exercises, you will likely have begun to glimpse the ineffable revolutions of the mechanisms of energy that weave themselves through the cosmos. These are glimpsed not with the eyes but with a sense beyond the physical body that originates from consciousness itself. These patterns are infinitely complex, and I use the word *glimpse* because at any given moment, we can see only a fraction of their movement. Humans are not omnivoyant beings.

This being said, perhaps the word *attunement* is best used to describe awakening to the patterns that turn the metaphorical wheels of the cosmos. Rather than viewing, we are learning to vibrate with the patterns of creation, which are at once musical and mathematical—resonant geometry in an infinite spiral. We learn to surf this spiral, to tune in and follow the chorus. This goes beyond simple intuition. It is harmony—living harmoniously and acting harmoniously. Though it may be reductive, we can see all actions as harmonious or discordant to the energetic flow around us, and we can, in our limited sphere of influence, equate harmonious action to kindness and discordant action to cruelty or perhaps simply lack of kindness.

Beyond this understanding, we can also learn to follow the patterns toward beneficent outcomes. When we are in tune, we may be led by voiceless thought to turn down a certain street, to call a certain friend at a certain time, and to make other small and seemingly unimportant decisions that may send ripples of causality dancing into the future in ways we may not comprehend, making differences we may never know about. This is important work. It is tuning in and always following the resonance of harmony. There is a tedious banality in cruelty and a predictability in selfishness to always do for itself, grasp for itself, and choose itself. In kindness, there is the impetus to work wonders simply for the beauty they may provide for others. Kindness is self-perpetuating in the same way that cruelty is self-consuming. A positive pattern adds exponentially, where a negative pattern subtracts in a similar way until it consumes itself; it is entropic. We always seek to add to the net sum of beauty. These are, of course, reductive ways of looking at something too complex to properly conceptualize in human thought.

As those who become aware of the patterns that weave the cosmos, in however limited a capacity, it is our duty to become agents of the harmonious song of existence. It is my belief that we are all receptive to these patterns in some way. However, if we are not consciously aware of them, we are liable to become lost in their propagation. When we walk through life as sleepwalkers, disconnected from our own inner worlds and uninterested in self-cultivation, we simply latch onto whatever patterns we attuned to in our formative years and follow them wherever they may take us—for good or ill. As magicians, we seek to avoid this course of action. We are always asking why we believe as we do, think as we do, and feel as we do. We seek to understand ourselves, and thus we achieve sovereignty over ourselves, refusing to simply march along through life, doing as we have always done simply because we have always done it.

As magicians, our total goal is to transcend to a state where we can better understand and harmonize with the patterns of existence and thus better serve the vast network of being that consists of all consciousness.

We do this through the pursuit of our art, often over many lifetimes, and through following the often indecipherable susurrus of the song of existence as it leads us to opportunities to use our art for beneficent outcomes.

Together we have learned to traverse the invisible world, whether we identify that world as a rich inner landscape or an nth dimensional overlay to our own physical existence. We have become comfortable in the liminal spaces of reality and in the company of the eidolons, with vestiges drifting by on the currents of causality and calcareous blockages dissolving at our will. There is an infinite landscape just beyond our visual perception. It is an innumerable host of intelligences in an intricate dance, and I hope to have helped you begin to be receptive to them.

I have done my best in the preceding pages to equip you with a set of specific exercises, a toolbox for developing your own exercises, and a heuristic launch point from which to explore your suppositions about magic and existence. I posit that the pursuit of magic should be a teleological one that builds itself around the meaning you personally glean from it. I cannot say that I did not have hesitations in drafting this work. I understand more than most the doors one can open when pursuing the high art that is magic. However, I also understand that, as a magician, I am charged with the duty of sharing any insights I may possess in the hopes they will be useful to someone somewhere. I entreat you to practice responsibly and with compassion toward yourself and others. Do not rush toward an answer; revel in the journey. Knowledge is like wine. It must mature to reach any real depth or complexity. Do not be so eager to find a conclusion that you end up with sour grape juice and regret. Rather, triple distill your theories until you are drunk on the grappa of understanding.

This book has been an exercise in imparting all of the basics of paneidolism, my own system of ritual magic, to you, the reader. I hope it has led you to keep your own working book full, and I most fervently hope it has provided you with more questions than it has answers. I hope to have lit a fire of curiosity rather than simply informed on a subject. While I have been able to participate in the pageantry of material society to date, my passion has always been this art, and I believe if more of us sought to understand beyond ourselves the world might be a kinder place for it.

I entreat you to go forth and discover. There is much to experience that will be unique to your own practice, and I encourage you to seek it out at your own pace and in your own time. There is much I have experienced that is unsuitable to share in a book tailored toward the introduction of this system to beginners, lest it flavor your own expectations, but I hope that you may discern some of it for yourself. I do hope to one day share those otherworldly journeys with you in another work—if this one in your hands gleans any interest toward further elaboration. For now, I ask that you record your own journeys that you might share them with your peers.

BIBLIOGRAPHY

Echols, Damien. *High Magick: A Guide to the Spiritual Practices that Saved My Life on Death Row*. Boulder, CO: Sounds True, 2022.

Gibran, Kahlil. *The Prophet*. New York: Alfred A Knopf, 1923.

Matsuo, Bashō. *Narrow Road to the Interior and Other Writings*. Translated by Sam Hamill. Boston: Shambhala Publications, 2006.

Odin, Steve. *Process Metaphysics and Hua-Yen Buddhism: A Critical Study of Cumulative Penetration vs. Interpenetration*. Albany, NY: State University of New York Press, 1982.

Regardie, Israel. *The Middle Pillar: A Co-Relation of the Principles of Analytical Psychology and the Elementary Techniques of Magic*. St. Paul, MN: Llewellyn Publications, 1970.

Sullivan, J. W. N. "Interviews with Great Scientists, Part VI." *Observer*, January 25, 1931.

To Write to the Author

If you wish to contact the author or would like more information about this book, please write to the author in care of Llewellyn Worldwide Ltd. and we will forward your request. Both the author and the publisher appreciate hearing from you and learning of your enjoyment of this book and how it has helped you. Llewellyn Worldwide Ltd. cannot guarantee that every letter written to the author can be answered, but all will be forwarded. Please write to:

J. R. Mascaro
℅ Llewellyn Worldwide
2143 Wooddale Drive
Woodbury, MN 55125-2989

Please enclose a self-addressed stamped envelope for reply,
or $1.00 to cover costs. If outside the U.S.A., enclose
an international postal reply coupon.

Many of Llewellyn's authors have websites with additional information and resources. For more information, please visit our website at http://www.llewellyn.com.